Heidegger,
Rorty,
and the
Eastern Thinkers

SUNY series in Chinese Philosophy and Culture

Roger T. Ames, editor

HEIDEGGER, RORTY, AND THE EASTERN THINKERS

A Hermeneutics of Cross-Cultural Understanding

Wei Zhang

STATE UNIVERSITY OF NEW YORK PRESS

Published by
State University of New York Press, Albany

© 2006 State University of New York

All rights reserved

Printed in the United States of America

For information, address State University of New York Press,
194 Washington Avenue, Suite 305, Albany, NY 12210-2384

Production by Judith Block
Marketing by Anne M. Valentine

Library of Congress Cataloging-in-Publication Data

Zhang, Wei, 1958–
    Heidegger, Rorty, and the Eastern thinkers : a hermeneutics of cross-cultural
understanding / Wei Zhang.
        p. cm. — (SUNY series in Chinese philosophy and culture)
    Includes bibliographical references and index.
    ISBN 0–7914–6751–1 (hardcover : alk. paper)
1. Philosophy, Comparative. 2. East and West. 3. Rorty, Richard. 4. Heidegger,
Martin, 1889–1976. I. Title. II. Series.

B799.Z38 2006
109—dc22

2005026769

ISBN–13: 978–0–7914–6751–0 (hardcover : alk. paper)

10 9 8 7 6 5 4 3 2 1

For Rob
—who shares the love and labor
in cross-cultural understanding

CONTENTS

Acknowledgments ix

Part I. *The Recurring East-West Hermeneutic Riddle* 1

 Introduction 3

Part II. *Richard Rorty's Correspondence with a Comparative Philosopher* 9

 1. The Question of Legitimacy of Comparative Philosophy 11
 2. Philosophy and Cultural Otherness 27

Part III. *Martin Heidegger's Dialogue with a Japanese Visitor* 45

 3. On the Way to a "Common" Language 47
 4. On the Way to a Cross-Cultural Hermeneutics 67

Part IV. *A Conceptual Dialogue with Heidegger's Text on Hermeneutics* 87

 5. Heidegger's Ontological Hermeneutics as a Worldview and World Encounter 89

Notes 109

Bibliography 121

Index 125

ACKNOWLEDGMENTS

This book evolved from a conference paper, "Heidegger and East-West Dialogue," delivered for the committee of International Society for Universal Dialogue at the Fourth World Conference at Jagiellonian University, Cracow, Poland, July 2001. The paper was later expanded and published in *Dao: A Journal of Comparative Philosophy*, and hence I am thankful to the journal editor for giving me permission to use a portion of the material in the current book. My continuing research on Heidegger's thought in East-West studies on the topics of language, hermeneutics, metaphysics, and technology constitutes a large portion of the book. The critical reading of Rorty's correspondence with Anindita N. Balslev on the disciplinary study of comparative philosophy and the notion of "cultural otherness" highlights some of the social concerns and political dimensions of the cross-cultural dialogue.

I extend my deep appreciation to the leading scholars in comparative philosophy and East Asian studies in this country as well as abroad: Roger Ames, professor and editor of the Chinese Philosophy and Culture series for the State University of New York Press and editor of *Comparative Philosophy*; Zhong-ying Cheng, professor and editor of *Journal of Chinese Philosophy*; Yong Huang, professor and editor of *Dao: A Journal of Comparative Philosophy*; and Jay Gaudling, professor of East Asian philosophy at York University, Ontario, Canada, for reviewing the book manuscript and providing insightful critiques. I would also like to thank my colleagues and graduate students for reading and discussing the manuscript with me at its various stages. Dr. Carlos Lopez, a Sanskrit scholar who recently joined our faculty in Religious Studies at the University of South Florida, had a chance to read the final version of the work and made important comments on the Sanskrit origin of Buddhist concepts.

I also heartily thank the State University of New York Press for preparing the manuscript for publication, and especially senior acquisition editor Nancy Ellegate for recognizing the significance of the work and persuasively presenting the project to SUNY Press's editorial board and to the outside scholarly community, and to production editor Judith Block and her staff for refining and turning the manuscript into a fine book.

It takes an author an extended time period and months and months of mental concentration from conceiving a book project to its eventual completion, which inevitably requires family members to understand the value of the work and lend moral support. Therefore, I extend my heartfelt appreciation to my husband, Rob Cooper, for his genuine concern for the work I do and his unconditional support and understanding for the time and energy it demands, and mostly, for his firm belief in me at times when I had doubts about myself.

PART I.
THE RECURRING
EAST-WEST
HERMENEUTIC RIDDLE

INTRODUCTION

The present study intends to engage a theoretical interest emerging in the academy in recent years in exploring the rich thematic ambiguity and philosophical problematic in the history of the East-West encounter. The question, have the East and West ever understood each other? becomes a recurring hermeneutic riddle that has never failed to claim the imagination of the best minds of the West—from Hegel, Husserl, and Heidegger to Richard Rorty, Huston Smith, and other critically-minded thinkers.

The perceived urgency to address the problematic nature of the East-West relation was captured by some of the most provocative remarks of contemporary leading thinkers. For instance, while the renowned religious scholar Huston Smith claimed that East and West are meeting is such an "understatement," the prominent pragmatist philosopher Richard Rorty, after attending the East-West Comparative Philosophy Conference at the University of Hawaii, argued the opposite: "the East and West did not meet" at all. For Smith, the East-West encounter in the present age is not facilitated merely by the advent of technology or driven by the curious minds of impatient intellectual curiosity. Rather, the meeting has evolved from a deep existential longing for an integrated world and a fuller humanity; and from being a "homesick for the world," even places where one has never been and suspects that one will never go. For Rorty, there is a lack of "a common option," among the East-West comparative philosophers, to discuss what are "the most immediate, forced, and lived issues."[1]

Representing the two opposing views on the subject matter, Smith's and Rorty's remarks nicely capture what John Clarke, author of *Oriental Enlightenment*, refers to as "an age-old ambivalence in the West's attitude towards the East." In his ambitious undertaking of the reconstruction of the last three hundred years' history of the East-West encounter since the age of enlightenment, Clarke offers an intriguing observation. That is, with the increasing contact between the two continents, facilitated by the cross-continental trade, colonial expansion, and the advent of technology, which have shortened the physical distance between the East and West, the Western perception toward its Other has become more ambivalent and perplexing. Clarke finds necessary to invoke Goethe's and Kipling's poetic expressions, articulated about a century ago to capture that ambivalence at the beginning of his book. While Goethe claimed: "He who knows himself and other will also recognize that East and West cannot be separated," Kipling disagreed: "Oh East is East, and West is West, and never the twain shall meet."[2] Is the speculation over such an East-West riddle as ancient as the actual encounter between the two continents themeslves?

Revisiting the question such as when the East becomes a problem for the West, some historians of ideas have recently pointed out that the West's problem with the East, or the East-West problematic, was certainly not only confined to the perception and expression of the present and the age of modernity.[3] In the classical period, the conflict between Greeks and Persians reported in Alexander's letters to Aristotle had already left the West with an impression that the East was a land of "despotic authority and barbaric splendor," and the cultural character of the Eastern peoples were "servile." Certainly, such impressions gave rise to the seventeenth century writer Montesquieu's contrast of European value for "liberty" with the Asian culture of servitude." The classical perception of the Orient continued to shape the medieval European perceptions and interpretations of its cultural Other. In both pilgrims' descriptions of the Islamic East or the "Scriptural East" and travelers' tales of the wonderland of Cathay, the East was portrayed as a mysterious land captured in sensual and exotic images. Locked in its ancient cultural caves, the mystic East refused to be penetrated by the rational mind of the West and hence remained hermeneutically perplexing; yet, the very Oriental perplexity, embodied in the cultural splendor and drastically different social landscapes, was persistently alluring and never failed to inspire the Western imagination and hermeneutic quest for meaning and significance. The European classical and medieval hermeneutical quest for meaning and understanding of what appeared to be unintelligible is described by Mary Campbell as the "dynamic struggle between the powers of language and the facts of life."[4] Asia, perceived as "both sufficiently 'known' (witnessed, experienced) and unknown (Other)," provided "the ground for such dynamic struggle," driven by a desire to map all that was satanic—of all the chaotic, fertile, multitudinous splendors... somewhere 'out there'" that "threatened the hegemony of its conscious values."[5] Campbell points out that it was through reading Alexander's letters to Aristotle that the Europeans first found "nourishment for its notions of 'monstrous' savagery,"[6] and it was through reading Marco Polo's writings to his fellow Italians that Europeans derived "the most balanced and lush of all medieval re-recreations of the East: the grotesque titillations of Wonders and the splendor and fertility of Paradise are here combined in a single comprehensive image."[7] By and large, both classical and medieval European depictions of the East from which it derives its self-image actually anticipated the paradoxical and conflicting expressions of the modern and contemporary ambivalence in the West's attitude toward its cultural Other, the East.

In the last half of the twentieth century, the opinion of the East-West relation has assumed a wide range of expressions. For some there have been on-going dialogues between the East and West for over three thousand years, and the meeting of the two is one of the most significant events in the history of mankind. For others, the East did not meet West and the perceived relation was only peripheral and ephemeral, and indeed, it was nothing more than the brief surge of the neo-Romantic movement of the 1960s or the fanciful dream of pop Nirvana as Clarke observed in his introduction to *Oriental Enlightenment*. Still for others, the East may have met with the West with some benefit, but there isn't anything significant that the West has learned from the East.[8] Thus, the East-West relation, if such a relation exists at all, was either dialogical and complementary, antagonistic and mutually exclusive, or asymmetrical and nonreciprocal. The attempts to reconcile and justify the respective dialogical, antagonistic, or asymmetrical positions have not been able to provide the solutions to the satisfaction of others. Hence, the question remains. Is there a relationship between the East and West?

Part II (chapters 1 and 2) examines the correspondence between Richard Rorty and Anindita N. Balslev and the ways in which they debated about the question of "legitimacy" of comparative philosophy, the curriculum reform, the related pedagogical issues, and ultimately, the West's self-understanding of the "origin" of philosophy and the subsequent disciplinary practice. If the notion of philosophy was an exclusively Greek concept and a genealogical linkage connecting "the good Uncle Kant and bad brother Derrida,"[9] by Rorty's definition, do Asians need philosophy the way the Europeans did? Is East-West comparative philosophy a legitimate academic discipline, or rather, have the East and West ever understood each other *philosophically* or *intellectually*? These questions thus bring out a larger philosophical and sociopolitical context in which the theme of cultural otherness, as Balslev calls it, the history of self-understanding of a discipline, and the process of transcribing the cultural difference into a disciplinary boundary are embedded.

Part III (chapters 3 and 4) discusses the dialogue between a Japanese visitor and Heidegger, who has disguised himself as an inquirer. The manner in which the dialogue was conducted assumes a different mode of cross-cultural engagement. While Rorty and Balslev are preoccupied with defending their own positions and winning the argument, Heidegger and his visitor attempt to listen rather than argue with each other, that encourages a deeper reflection and longer discussion of some philosophical questions. First, if language is not merely a linguistic construct of spoken and written signs, but an ontological property, or "the House of Being," in Heidegger's metaphor, could the East and the West strike a common understanding of each other's languages and traditions? Could cross-cultural understanding being attempted if communication were to depend on a translation mechanism—to convert one language into the other? Second, if hermeneutics is not to be understood merely as methodology of interpretation, as Heidegger argues, but that of a process of simultaneous preservation and retrieval of the message of one's historical destiny, could in the twentieth century encounter between German and Japanese thinkers constitute an authentic hermeneutic relationship?

Part IV (chapter 5) is the conceptual dialogue between the author of the present study with Heidegger's primary text on hermeneutics and phenomenology, first delivered as a lecture series in the summer of 1923. To engage in a dialogue with Heidegger is to think with him by following a path that is both familiar and foreign, near and far, illuminating and perplexing. However, the traveling experience is ultimately rewarding, since Heidegger allows his interlocutor to transgress the limits that his thinking imposes upon itself, which eventually leads to the opening up of broader intellectual horizon where one could see one's own world fusing with that of the other and the possibility of walking "on the boundary of what is originally boundless with the other," as he suggested to his interlocutor. The conceptual dialogue with Heidegger's text, *Ontology—The Hermeneutics of Facticity*, would thus promote such an encounter from which emerges similar worldviews that both see the movement of world-encounter as the meeting between temporal and particular beings, beings being-in-the-world and being-with-the-others, without depending on a theo-metaphysical presence and a subject-object schema.

The present study takes its methodological departure from the existing scholarship that views the East and West as the "mighty opposites" of the two ends of the Old World or different stages of the evolving World History and Spirit that calls for a higher dialectic synthesis—a Hegelian thesis; but rather, it treats the East-West relation as a hermeneutic riddle. A riddle is not simply a mathematical problem waiting to be solved or a practical difficulty that calls for a technical solution. Nor is it a puzzle that can be figured out by putting all the pieces together. A riddle resembles a Zen koan that baffles or perplexes, that defies logical explanation. Refusing to be exhausted by rational interpretive activities, the koan constantly engages the listeners who are listening to its moral message; as each time it speaks, it speaks anew.

PART II.
RICHARD RORTY'S
CORRESPONDENCE
WITH A COMPARATIVE
PHILOSOPHER

Chapter 1

THE QUESTION OF LEGITIMACY OF COMPARATIVE PHILOSOPHY

> ... the lack of conversation between India and the
> West is most glaring among philosophers.
> —Anindita N. Balslev, ed., *Cultural Otherness*, p. 10

> ... comparative philosophy is more than an empty
> gesture, a skilled complement that creates more awk-
> wardness than collegiality.
> —Richard Rorty, in Anindita N. Balslev, ed.,
> *Cultural Otherness*, p. 9

In spite of his strong conviction that what we call philosophy today is a Greek concept and hence an exclusively European practice, Richard Rorty oftentimes surprises his audiences with his presence at the East-West philosophy conferences, engaging in the dialogues or argument with comparative philosophers whose work reaches beyond the textual boundary of the West. Most recently, Rorty attended an international symposium on "Rorty Pragmatism and Chinese Philosophy," held in East China Normal University in Shanghai, China in July 2004, committing himself to the discussion about American-Chinese pragmatist connections.[1] Traveling from conference to conference, Rorty delivered papers and made comments about non-Western intellectual traditions, raising issues about the practice of comparative philosophy. Not only did Rorty engage in face-to-face dialogues, he also had correspondence with non-Western thinkers, writing book reviews for the publications in East-West comparative philosophy. Rorty's correspondence with Anindita N. Balslev, who, unlike Rorty, chose to work with the

Western and Indian texts simultaneously, will be the focus of the discussion of the present chapter.

The correspondence was initiated by Balslev, who responded to a conference paper that Rorty delivered at the Sixth East-West Comparative Philosophy Conference held at the University of Hawaii in 1989. In the paper, Rorty challenged the legitimacy of the discipline of comparative philosophy and the perceived relevance of Martin Heidegger to the East-West "intercultural comparison." The main thrust of Rorty's argument was that since philosophy is a uniquely Greek concept and a specialized form of intellectual inquiry instituted in the Western academy, any comparison of philosophy can create more awkwardness than collegiality among fellow philosophers.[2] Balslev disagreed with Rorty by suggesting that every historical culture has an intellectual tradition or traditions dedicated to the search for the "ultimate" questions of human existence and knowledge—either in India or Greece, thus the study of philosophy as an academic subject can certainly be comparative. Politely protesting Rorty's attempt to undermine the role not only of comparative philosophy as an academic discipline, but indeed, that of philosophy itself, Balslev appealed to the contemporary urgency to implement a "theory" and "program" to back up the increasing interest in cross-cultural studies of the subject of philosophy. The subsequent exchange of letters was edited by Balslev and published under the title *Cultural Otherness: Correspondence with Richard Rorty*, first by the Indian Institute of Advanced Studies in 1989 and later by the American Academy of Religion, Scholars Press in 1991.

Balslev detected an ethnocentrism in Rorty's definition of philosophy and suspected that it is the "theme of cultural otherness" and the category of the Other in general that had prevented academic philosopher's such as Rorty, from participating in the cross-cultural conversation that continued to perpetuate "the East-West asymmetries in academic exchange."[3] Rorty rejected Balslev's accusation on pragmatic grounds. He pointed out that the only practical way to balance the asymmetry is to create a new social 'economic order' that reverses the "flow of money and power." Only then could one solve the problem of convincing Western youths to take an interest in the subject matter of the East.

Toward the end of the correspondence, there emerged an impasse that seems to have frustrated both Rorty and Balslev. Rorty remarked that he was not even sure how to go around it. He also made a similar comment after he attended the Hawaii conference, that he felt strongly that "the East and West did not meet," and there was an absence of "common options to discuss, options…which William James called 'live, immediate and forced.'"[4] Balslev almost agreed with Rorty there. She stated that it never seems to be so difficult for her to cross over a "boundary."[5] Her questions to Rorty were thus: Was the *cultural* boundary between the "insider" and "outsider" of a given intellectual tradition so *conceptually* conditioned that it automatically transcribed itself into a *disciplinary* boundary? Was it always necessary to impose a priori judgments for the comparative studies of different intellectual traditions?[6]

Needless to say, those unresolved questions further perpetuated the riddlelike East-West relation that we had discussed in the introduction. It seems that, one way to make some sense out of this seemingly unfruitful exchange between Rorty and Balslev is to take a close look at the ways in which some of the arguments were laid out and developed and how their respective positions were informed by a specific body of knowledge and a personal interest and background. And yet, the lack of discussion and an understanding of each other's knowledge formation and personal background anticipated the failure of the cross-cultural communication. To bring out the overlooked issues and illuminate the missing background that informs the respective positions that they tried to defend may shed some light to a number of issues that are of immediate importance to philosophy's self-understanding; the future development of its curriculum, and a general understanding of the cultural and intellectual topics of one's Other. For instance, we will try to demonstrate how a philosophical attitude that was developed in Western academies over the centuries had informed Rorty's discomfort to engage in what he termed the "intercultural comparison." Conversely, we will try to trace the development of a more recent comparative scholarship that challenged the self-understanding of philosophy sanctified by the canonical thinkers of the West, which seems to deeply implicate Balslev's position and argument.

Philosophy, Essentialism, and the "Intercultural Comparison"–Rorty's argument

Rorty's aversion to comparative philosophy as a disciplinary practice in the academy of the West was first expressed as an aversion to philosophy itself. In his conference paper, "Philosophy, Novelists, and Intercultural Comparison: Heidegger, Kundera, and Dickens," Rorty challenged the perceived relevance of Western philosophy and Heidegger to East-West comparison, which seemed to be prevalent among the conference participants at the Hawaii meeting. The main thrust of Rorty's criticism of philosophy as a Western intellectual tradition and disciplinary study is that it is inherently "essentialist." Philosophical essentialism, among other things, has reduced the complexity, diversity, and intricate details of the lifeworld into abstract concepts. This kind of reductive essentialism may be useful in the development of a mathematical language to describe the "microstructures behind confusing macro-structures," but proves to be useless in searching for a law or universal pattern underlining social histories and world cultures, according to Rorty.[7] In an echo to a postmodern call for a deconstruction of the Western metaphysical tradition, Rorty proceeded to undermine the tendency to "theorize about human affairs,"[8] and abstract from human life affairs "the essence, form, underlining structure," and , the ineffable Other.[9]

In Rorty's view, Heidegger's work typified such a philosophical essentialism. Whereas Plato looked down, Heidegger gazed back; both men attempted to search for something that is wholly Other than the West itself in order to overcome its tradition. Instead of looking at the world as it is lived or as it is unfolding, Heidegger directed his gaze back to remote Greek antiquity, based upon which, as Heidegger hoped, a social Utopia of a fourfold world of heaven, earth, gods, and mortals may be recaptured and projected onto the present and future. Under an equalizing philosophical gaze, Heidegger sees, as Rorty described, no distinction between "Stalin's Russia and Roosevelt's America," since they only represent "surface perturbation, distraction from essence by accidents," and "metaphysically speaking," they are the same.[10] Hence, in Rorty's assessment, Heidegger's ambition to overcome the tradition—metaphysics and technology—of the West had actually failed to accomplish its objective. Not only did it blur the distinction of fundamentally different sociopolitical realities, it also created a new type of metaphysical thinking, a thinking of an ancient antiquity as a primordial reality standing beyond and above everyday life. The return to a primordial reality, among other things, sustained an existence of a social class of ascetic priests, including Heidegger himself, whose obsession with purity and cleanliness and refusal to muddle with everyday human affairs in turn facilitated a sense of self-hatred among Western intellectuals and a pervasive "social pessimism" in Western societies. Thus to view Heidegger's words as "the last message of the West," and his work

as paradigmatic of Western philosophical reflection was counterpro-
ductive, if not entirely misleading.

Thus concluded, Rorty advised against using Heidegger's work
with Eastern texts and with the practice of comparative philosophy in
general. The latter, conducted within the framework of the essentialism, usually compares the entire intellectual traditions of the East and
West, encouraging the "adaptations of a single transcultural character
type to different environments."[11] Putting the West "as a whole," in
contrast to "the rest of the world as a whole," comparative philosophy is
hardly "a royal road to intercultural comparison," but rather, an easy way
of out the difficulties facing the disciplinary practice.[12]

Rorty's critical attitude toward the discipline of comparative philosophy is persistent. A year prior to the East-West comparative philosophy in Hawaii, Rorty had explicitly expressed his skepticism about the
possibility of comparing Eastern and Western philosophical texts in his
book review on Larson and Deutsch's is edited collection, *Interpreting
across Boundaries: New Essays in Comparative Philosophy*. Rorty stated,
"comparative philosophy," understood as "applying the term 'philosophy' to Asian books" is only "an empty gesture, a stilled complement
that creates more awkwardness that collegiality."[13] The gesture signifies
a false complement that assumes Asians have what the Europeans
called philosophy and that there is a need in Asia for philosophy to be
taught in the way that the Europeans did in the modern universities.
Therefore, one should not be afraid to be accused of being "a cultural
imperialist," but be courageous enough to reassert an old question in
"honest bewilderment," is there philosophy in Asia? Although, the
question may be taken to imply that Asians are not intellectually
mature, yet, one may simply defend one's position by stating that such a
question was posed only to find out if Asians need philosophy the way
that the Europeans do.[14]

Rorty indeed threw the question back to Balslev when she invited
Rorty, in one of her letters, to think along with her in terms of how to
build some theoretical or philosophical programs in support of comparative study of the subject matter of philosophy. Rorty asked her to reflect
first whether Asians have had a need to teach various Western philosophers in their departments of philosophy and whether the Western categories of philosophy were useful to organize the Indian texts.
Specifically, Rorty asked, "Have Asians had any of the needs which have
led Western universities to teach Seneca, Ockham, Hume, and Husserl in
the same department?"[15] Could the Western categories of metaphysics,

epistemology, and logic be employed to classify the classical Indian texts? If so, Rorty frankly admitted, he would be disappointed.[16]

However, there is an alternative way to conduct East-West comparison, if Balslev were to insist on such a practice. For instance, Rorty recommended, comparative philosophers could supplement the intercultural dialogue on the theories with that of the "antitheory."[17] That is, they could use the narrative traditions of the West, such as literature and journalism, to conduct East-West study. The nineteenth century realist novels were a much better genre of writing that the West could extend to the East. Unlike philosophers, novelists did a much better job of portraying modern Western societies; unlike Heidegger, Dickens gave a more reliable account of the realities of Western or European cultures. In vivid details and with a good sense of humor, Dickens provides a "diversity of points of view" and "a plurality of descriptions of the same events."[18] Whereas philosophical essentialism attempted to retain the distinction between reality and appearance, essence and phenomenon, literary pluralism blurred the distinction between the seeming opposites. Whereas Heidegger projected a utopian "pastoral" world where "life is given shape by its relationship to the primordial fourfold," Dickens presented a world filled with "a crowd of eccentrics rejoicing in each other's idiosyncrasies, curious for novelty rather than nostalgic for primordiality."[19] Thus, in Rorty's view, one finds in Dickens's literary world a "democratic utopia," where "tolerance and curiosity replaced the quest for truth and the greatness…the admirable intellectual virtues" of the modern West.[20]

Could Rorty Point a Way Out of the Difficulties of Intercultural Comparison?

Anyone who has read Rorty's philosophical papers produced over the last two decades may have an appreciation of his persistent effort to undermine the essentialist and metaphysical thesis that has dominated the thinking of generations of philosophers in the Western academy. Rorty's critical assessment of philosophy—an insider's view of the inherent problems of its tradition and discipline—could be a welcoming invitation for the outsiders to contribute to the philosophy's self-reflection and self-criticism. For instance, one may expect that Rorty could perhaps shed some light on how the philosophical essentialism had negatively affected the study of Eastern ideas in the Western academy and why the attempt to apply Western categories to "name" non-

Western texts could be considered a form of "epistemological violence," as deconstructionist thinker Jacques Derrida termed it. According to Derrida, such a naming practice may obscure and even distort the historical and cultural specificities of the non-Western texts and traditions. If Western philosophical categories such as logic, epistemology, and metaphysics are inappropriate for classifying Eastern texts and canons, could Rorty help identify a set of new conceptual categories that are mutually intelligible to both Indian and Western thinkers in terms of organizing and understanding the history of ideas, texts, and scriptures of one another? How else would philosophers in the West get to know the way that Indians go about pursuing the answers to the ultimate questions about life, human bondage, and liberation, discussed between fathers and sons, husbands and wives at home, and in the market? Balslev asked. Her ultimate question posed to Rorty is that, "Does "*darśana* or *ānvīkṣikī* in the Sanskritic tradition" correspond to "what is called *philosophia* in the west?"[21] It appears that Balslev had sincerely hoped that Rorty could join her in the self-reflection of the disciplinary position, exploring some methodological questions in the newly emerged critical juncture of comparative philosophy.

Rorty indeed responded to the invitation, as we mentioned earlier. He had initially suggested substituting theory with antitheories in doing East-West comparison in his conference paper. Rorty's appeal to an "aestheticism," echoing with the voices of other postmodern thinkers before him, seems to rest on the perceived power of the literary genre to free the modern Western mind from the domination of metaphysical thinking. For instance, Nietzsche, Heidegger, and others once used either poetry or prose as a way to write out of the confinement of philosophical essentialism. However, neither in the conference paper nor his subsequent correspondence to Balslev, did Rorty explore any textual strategy to facilitate such an experiment. One expects if Rorty were truly interested in helping to develop the alternative textual strategies for intercultural comparison, he would be able to outline some possibility to endorse "a program for philosophy as narrative" that facilitates "such pragmatic virtues" as "tolerance and comfortable togetherness," as Balslev quoted him.[22] Apparently, Rorty showed no interest in convincing the conference participants, and later, his correspondent, as to how a Victorian literary genre was more *accessible* for comparative philosophers with non-Western backgrounds and why Dickens's writing of Victorian England in the nineteenth century was a more realistic representation of modern Western societies than Heidegger's philosophical reflection produced between the two World Wars in the twentieth century. For one may well argue that philosophy or literature, written in abstract or concrete terms, are simply two different genres of writing describing various aspects of human life experiences. Balslev indeed challenged his emphasis on literary writing and pointed out that there are certain texts that could not easily be classified as either philosophy or literature, and that the overlapping of different genres of writing is actually a common practice in the postmodern writing world. Hence, Rorty's preference for literature over philosophy could merely be a matter of his personal taste for a certain genre of writing over others. Otherwise, Rorty would have to explain why did he personally choose to remain an academic philosopher and to continue to speak and write from this framework but encourage comparative philosophers to substitute philosophy with literature. Another seemingly confusing message that Rorty sent out concerns the status of Heidegger in the canon of philosophy. One cannot make any sense why did Rorty, while ranking Heidegger as one of the three most original thinkers in the twentieth century, decided to undermine his work in a cross-cultural setting, and in the company of comparative philosophers?[23]

Comparative Philosophy as a Way Out of Philosophical Essentialism—Balslev's Solution

Balslev certainly agreed with Rorty that in the West philosophical essentialism had managed to reduce the lifeworld and daily pursuits into abstract concepts and objects for theoretical reflection; and that the traditional metaphysical thinking and its modern epistemological assumptions need to be critically assessed and undermined. The practice of comparative philosophy, remaining in the grip of the essentialism, may have very well propagated a transcultural character, which certainly calls for a deconstruction. In her preface to the *Correspondence*, Balslev warned her colleagues in the comparative disciplines to resist the temptation of a priori judgments and "transcultural interpretive strategies"[24] in their interpretation of the "overlapping contents" and "incommensurable otherness of the other traditions."[25]

However, the disagreement of how philosophy could be rescued from the grip of metaphysics polarized their positions. In Rorty's opinion, philosophy as a discipline in the West is declining—it is losing its "efficacy and status." Perhaps, it is due to its inherent essentialist nature, or to the emergence of the new disciplinary studies and genres of writing. Rorty's remark resonates with the postmodern call to "end" philosophy. While Heidegger had claimed that only if we were to end metaphysics or ontology, the underlining structure of philosophy, could the thinking begin, Derrida asserted that only if we were to close the book, would we be able to open the text.

Unlike Rorty, Balslev still believed in the cardinal importance of philosophy. It is the repository from which the major torrent of the intellectual and cultural enquiries emerged and is still emerging.[26] As such, ending philosophy or doing away with philosophical essentialism would lead to a cultural and intellectual nihilism. A more constructive alternative to renew the rigor of the discipline, Balslev suggested, would be to enlarge its intellectual horizon and extend its monologue with the Self to a dialogue with the Other—the intellectual traditions of the East. Practicing philosophy comparatively and dialogically is both theoretically and practically plausible. Historically, there was no evidence suggesting that any intellectual traditions had closed up their conceptual horizons, even if they might have achieved a complete self-understanding. In the West, Balslev tells us, the comparison of Eastern and Western ideas can be traced back to the early "intellectual adventure in the Indian subcontinent," and to certain individuals' efforts to "search for philosophy" outside the boundaries of the Western canon.[27] Over time, comparative philosophy established itself as an academic discipline, gaining its methodological maturity and recognition by other disciplines through detailed historical scholarship and analyses, despite some skepticism of its legitimacy.[28] On the other side of the world, for instance, it is India's encounter with the modern West that had given rise to the practice of comparative philosophy in the Indian Continent. European ideas and philosophical systems not only provided analytical tools for reconstructing the classical texts, but awoke a sense of self-pride of India's intellectual and spiritual past. The methodological enrichment and self-affirmation of the value of its cultural heritage eventually yielded to the most productive period in Indian intellectual history—the Indian Renaissance. In her own experience, Balslev testified that the opportunities to be exposed to non-Indian traditions and to be able to work with Western and Indian texts simultaneously, were intellectual fruitful and personally rewarding.

The practice of comparative philosophy not only helps with overcoming the pitfall of philosophy's essentialism, hence revitalizing the tradition and discipline; it may serve as a forum for a broader academic understanding of each other's traditions and hence a way to balance the

East-West asymmetry in the academy. The attempt to correct unbalanced circulation of ideas and texts between the East and West is urgent. Balslev cited the influential Indian thinker, Mehta, to back up her claim. Mehta had pointed out that there was a long-standing, noreciprocal relation between Indian political theorists and their Western counterparts; and that it is Indian thinkers who took the concerns of their Western colleagues seriously by making efforts to master the languages necessary to understand the Western philosophical texts, but not the other way around. Echoing Mehta, Balslev suggested the situation in the department of political science actually mirrors the Western academy as a whole, and that the lack of interest and commitment to the understanding of one's Other have impoverished the individual capacity to "sustain its part in this dialogue" in the West.[29]

According to Balslev, the lack of exposure and knowledge of one's intellectual Other in the academy also impaired a social and public understanding of one another among the diverse groups of peoples and hence, contributed negatively to the ongoing cultural stereotyping and social segregation. For instance, it is generally regarded that the Eastern notion of time is cyclical, in contrast to that of the Judeo-Christian view of time as linear. The time metaphors of the circle and arrow have carried some negative social implications, among them, the perception of Eastern histories and societies as static or unchanging and hence, lacking in progress and even the possibility for salvation.

Thus, for Balslev, the practice of comparative philosophy not only carries an educational mission but a social responsibility. Appealing to the social and moral responsibility of professional philosophers, Balslev urged them to familiarize themselves with their non-native traditions, contributing their knowledge to the ongoing process of socialization and cross-cultural education of the general public. She claimed, "philosophers matter; their ideas are of consequences." The more daring they are to cross the boundaries of their native traditions, "the better for the intellectual life of the future generation."[30] Balslev's position in this regard does not differ from that of Rorty. One recalls that in his Hawaii conference paper, Rorty had spoken against the ascetic priests or Heideggerian type of philosophers who were socially disengaged and politically indifferent and strongly encouraged his philosophical colleagues to locate their intellectual exercises in a larger context of social concerns.

Rorty and Balslev's Dispute over Philosophy Curriculum

The similar understanding between Rorty and Balslev on the social role that a responsible philosopher should play did not lead to an agreement on what kind of change was needed in the academy to not only renew the discipline of philosophy, but also to help with the social and cultural integration of segregated societies at large. In Balslev's view, the first step is to reform the philosophy curriculum at institutions of higher learning. The need for curriculum reform is self-explanatory in Balslev's view. For Western educational institutions at large are preoccupied with "national narratives," which does not help facilitate the "global interdependent societies in any honest sense."[31] In her judgment, the core curriculum of philosophy typically reflects such a preoccupation. Compared to other disciplines, "the lack of conversation between India and the West is most glaring among philosophers."[32] Efforts to reach out for intellectual resources outside the Western canon are rare, and there is "a dearth"[33] of representations of Eastern texts in the department of philosophy. The inadequate representation of non-Western texts in the philosophy curriculum, in turn, perpetuates a "parochial" attitude that ignores "the discourses of other cultures" altogether.[34] The message that Balslev attempted to convey is clear. The new generation should be "socialized differently" and the capacity for thinking globally should not only be a catchword but an educational credit. Non-Western intellectual resources and traditions need to be added on and integrated into the curriculum. To pursue a curriculum reform, Balslev called for a "conscious planning and commitment," as well as the participation of academic philosophers who "customarily work within the bounded space of their own traditional disciplinary concerns."[35]

Theoretically, Rorty agreed with Balslev's assessment. He stated that "the West is a more compulsory subject for people in the East but not vice versa." It is correct to say that "we in the West have not exerted ourselves enough to get relevant information" about the East; and "it is we in the West who are impoverished by our failure to sustain our part in "the East-West dialogue.[36] Therefore, it is reasonable to require Western students to learn more of the non-Western curriculum and to become more involved in building of a "global community."[37]

Yet, Rorty quickly changed his mind *as* he paused to reflect some pedagogical problems. For instance, how do we implement a comparative curriculum in the department of philosophy? Quantitatively, unlike the Western textual tradition that is relatively "homogenous and mono-lithic"—such as nineteenth-century curriculum composed of "the Christian-scientific-technological" traditions—Eastern texts contained in the multiple sources in the "Islamic tradition, two great Indian tradi-tions, a Chinese and a Japanese tradition" are massive in numbers, Rorty argued in his letter to Balslev. Given such a large body of texts, how much territory does comparative philosophy curriculum need to accom-modate Eastern texts? Moreover, there are significant thematic gaps to be reconciled if the Eastern texts are to be inserted into the Western canon. Rorty asked, how could Eastern texts be inserted into Western canon without creating "pointless hurdles to be leaped over" by Western students?[38] In other words, how could Eastern texts, the Upanishads and the Analects, for instance, be added to the philosophy curriculum with-out furnishing students with any social and historical background knowledge of ancient India and China, where those texts were com-posed and produced?

Rorty imagined that a solution to those perceived pedagogical problems perhaps lies with the possibility of importing some native intellectuals to the West, who may then supply some missing back-ground knowledge of Eastern texts and thus bridge the thematic gaps. Yet such a solution does not seem plausible either. For to implement such a practice would cause a "brain drain" of the intellectual resources of non-Western societies, given the fact that in the East there may not yet be enough cultural resources to engage in *"mission civilizatrice."*[39] Talking about the civilization mission, let us think about the situation in nineteenth-century colonial Africa and India, Rorty suggested. Those were the times when young people were forced to take courses in Plato and Shakespeare without having any sense of what to do with them except for passing civil exams to obtain better jobs in the colonial government. Today, how could we justify to Western youth that they need to take courses in the subjects of the East?

With Rorty, the pedagogical problems thus translated themselves into ideological ones. The term *mission civilizatrice* that he uses cannot help but communicate a negative meaning of imposition and indoctri-nation, given the context of modern colonialism. As Rorty himself real-ized that the nineteenth century was "the great period of imperialism and…indoctrination of non-Westerns with the Western ideas."[40] Given the self-appointed mission to civilize other peoples went hand-in-hand with the aggressive political and economic domination that had become an out-of-date practice; it is perplexing for us to see why

Rorty chose to review Balslev's call for an East-West comparative philosophy program in the light of colonialism and *mission civilizatrice*. What did Rorty imply when he drew a parallel between a comparative philosophy program today and the colonial curriculum of the past centuries? For Balslev and other critics of Rorty, his blurring of the distinction between the two sets of historical contexts that informed the colonial educational agenda and that of the comparative curriculum today, respectively, is likely to invite serious criticism. He could be blamed for his oversight on the respective historical and political realities to say the least, and possibly a "mild ethnocentrism," or "secondary narcissism," or even "strong imperialism" at the worst.[41]

Are Philosophical Questions Disguised Political Questions?

So far as we can see, Rorty did not take on the question that Balslev invited him to address, nor did he attempt to elaborate on any textual strategies as alternatives to the essentialist approach to the East-West comparison. Instead, Rorty dismissed most of Balslev's questions based on a pragmatist stance.

Reasserting his pragmatic tradition, Rorty declared in his reply to Balslev that what Balslev had identified as philosophical questions are actually "disguised political questions." For instance, the discussions about the Other and that of identity and difference and so on frequently debated among philosophers in both the West and India, as Balslev would like him to believe, are not genuine philosophical questions but rather a function of "human interests."[42] Similarly, Rorty pointed out, the perceived East-West asymmetry in the academic exchange that Balslev would like him to address is not philosophical but a direct reflection of the unbalanced distribution of material wealth and power between the Eastern and Western worlds.

Assuming that all the philosophical problems could be settled in pragmatic terms, would it be more productive for comparative philosophers to talk politics instead of philosophy? Rorty suggested, indeed, that instead of talking about reforming the philosophy curriculum, perhaps it would be more constructive to discuss the plans for social and political reforms of Eastern societies. For instance, instead of attempting to create a new "cultural order," would it be more practical to discuss the ways of implementing an "economical order" with which the flow of money and power between the East and West can be reversed and with which members of the Eastern societies would be allowed to pursue their individual potentials and eliminate "the struggles between the haves and have-nots"?[43]

To talk about politics, the new economic order, and the ways of redistributing money and power, one needs to consider how the Western model of modernization may be applied to the non-Western societies. In Rorty's judgment, Europe or the West has developed the optimal model for modernization and social progresses. The liberal democracy and technology greatly reduced human suffering and maximized personal happiness. What Rorty told Balslev in his letter is that what had prepared the West for the social progress was secularization. Secularization allowed the Western man to shift his relation with the historical and atemporal being, that is, God, truth, to that of the temporal, that is, the one between "man and his descendants." This shift enabled Western societies to pursue daily happiness and encourage the accumulation of material wealth. By implication, Rorty seemed to suggest that the societies that did not go through such a secularization process, its members are still relating themselves to gods, spirits, or heroes in order to bear what is unbearable in everyday conditions such as poverty and inequality. In the latter case, there will always be a need for and dependence on a superhuman being and the presence of ascetic priests. By comparison and contrast, Rorty explicitly stated that modern Western societies signify "a culture of hope," whereas their Eastern counterparts signify a "culture of endurance."[44]

Rorty's proposal to resolve all the philosophical problems by pragmatic or political means did not persuade Balslev to change her orientation and conviction. She argued that it is very dubious to assume today that the Western model of modernization can be directly applied to the non-Western societies and that non-Western peoples may desire modernization but not necessarily Westernization. Looking retrospectively, since independence from the colonial yoke, Eastern societies face very different social historical circumstances in a postcolonial world than their Western counterparts found themselves in at the beginning stages of modernization. The political leaders of these non-Western societies, such as Gandhi and others, also perceived some inherent problems and pitfalls of the Western Empire, and hence were motivated to look for alternatives to modernize their young nations.

We can certainly tell that Rorty's statement about the process of secularization and the reduction of religion to a mechanism for coping with poverty and inequality, or a means to sanctify the endurance for human suffering, would be challenged from both the Western and

Eastern fronts. For some social thinkers in the West may argue with him that, with the advent of secular humanism and, the successful accumulation of material wealth, and technological power, the Western part of the world has not been able to eliminate some serious social problems, such as urban poverty, human suffering, social injustice and inequality, racism, and other catastrophes witnessed by two World Wars. On the Eastern front, scholars of Eastern religions may point out that Rorty's assumption about the role religion plays in Eastern societies betrays a significant misunderstanding of a basic tenet of their religious traditions. They may want to inform Rorty that most Eastern religious traditions—Buddhism, Confucianism, and Daoism, to name a few—did not evolve around an ahistorical and atemporal being in the first place. From the time of the very conception of these traditions, there had been a strong humanistic tendency and approach to the so-called ultimate questions of the world and human conditions, and the religious practices have never exclusively been oriented toward a creator God, or supernatural being. For instance, Buddhism started out with a rejection of the pre-Buddhist notion of Brahman/Atman—a theo-metaphysical presence, and proposed to see the world as co-originated and mutually conditioned one made of physical, mental, and psychological events (*dharmas*). In fact, the seemingly overly humanistic orientation in Buddhist and Confucian traditions are sometimes perceived as religions without God or not religions at all by some Western scholars of religions!

The Impasse between Rorty and Balslev

Toward the end of *Correspondence*, readers can clearly see an "impasse" being developed between the correspondents, despite great efforts on both sides to achieve a cross-cultural understanding. For Balslev, the lack of intellectual dialogue between Western and Eastern philosophers are most glaring; and the East-West asymmetry in the Western academy is "conspicuous."[45] For Rorty, there is no "uncontroversial starting point to compare different intellectual systems,"[46] and what is regarded as philosophy is simply a Greek concept. Whereas Balslev argued about the importance of understanding the intellectual systems of the Other—what is beyond one's own native traditions, and the necessity of an East-West comparative curriculum as an integral part of a larger enterprise of global integration, Rorty perceived the advocacy of comparative philosophy and the requirment of Western students to learn more about non-Western books virtually the same as perpetuating the colonial curriculum that indoctrinates one group of people with that of the other.

It seems the overemphasis on the political and social dimensions of the East-West encounter had created a hostile dialogue environment, in which, each sees the argument of the other as being implicated by a coercive power that intended to challenge the conviction of oneself. The hostility in turn gives rise to a self-defense mechanism that prevented both sides from seeing the position of the other and from joining efforts to explore the possibility of communicating of not only pedagogical and academic but social and cultural.

To get around this impasse so as to make some sense of this seemingly unfruitful exchange, we may suggest first to Rorty that not all pedagogical problems are necessarily ideological by nature, and that education about other cultures cannot always be reduced to the means to fulfill a practical vocational end. The interest of young people in learning about other cultures and texts—either Shakespeare for Asian students or Confucius for Western youths are not always motivated by practical concerns to pass exams, get good jobs, or to be credited as multicultural. The equation is not valid simply because the pursuit of intellectual interest is not always *proportionally* conditioned by political trends and the perceived practical utility, and therefore, the changing of the political and economical dynamic alone may not rectify the academic East-West asymmetry. Similarly, we may remind Balslev that a program does not always need to have an institutional endorsement to promote and justify its legitimacy of a curriculum committee to make the non-Western subjects a prerequisite for the students to take. For the comparative study of a variety of academic subjects, including philosophy, is already an existence in the academy in the West; and Western education today is not always preoccupied with only the national narrative as she has claimed. To draw a temporary closure of our discussion on the first part of the *Correspondence*, we may suggest that the interest in learning about one's intellectual Other and the academic curriculum cannot always be facilitated by either a political economy or an institution in the form of a Department, program, or curriculum committee. On the contrary, it is usually the latter that responds to the challenge and demand of the former. What then are the "real" issues that Rorty and Balslev are debating?

Chapter 2

PHILOSOPHY AND CULTURAL OTHERNESS

> does *darsana*... in the Sanscritic tradition correspond
> at all to what is called *philosophia* in the West?
> —Anindita N. Balslev, preface to *Cultural Otherness*:
> *Correspondence with Richard Rorty*

> [Philosophy is] simply "a genealogical linkage con-
> necting certain past figures with present figures." It is
> an "ancestral relation of overlapping fibers."
> —Richard Rorty, *Cultural Otherness: Correspondence*
> *with Richard Rorty*

The debate between Rorty and Balslev about the discipline of comparative philosophy and curriculum reform eventually yields to a serious dispute about the nature or origin of philosophy itself and other more
primary questions. For instance, in what historical and cultural context
could we discuss the nature or origin of philosophy today? Is it a universal form of inquiry, common to all historical cultures in pursuing
answers to ultimate questions, as Balslev perceived; or is philosophy a
specific practice, a family business conducted by genealogically linked
family members, as Rorty defined it? Is the category of the Other a significant working concept in relation to the disciplinary practice of philosophy? And since *when*, and indeed *how*, has the cultural difference
been translated and transcribed into a disciplinary boundary?
Ultimately, if the very origin of philosophy is called into dispute, could
the East and West understand each other *intellectually*?

Apparently, for Rorty, the rectification of the name for philosophy in
terms of its origin, history, and current status is a serious task for academic

27

philosophers. Rorty has spent a concentrated amount of energy in the last two decades of his academic life to challenge the conventional self-understanding of philosophy in the West. According to him in the Platonic tradition, philosophy is premised on a form of essentialism—the study of Being as a constant presence, known as metaphysics. In a number of philosophical papers, Rorty reclaimed his pragmatist heritage to deconstruct the metaphysical tendency that underlies philosophy's self-understanding. Engaging himself in a long-term battle with a wide range of positions and perspectives of the canonical philosophers who had, to a different degree, defended the so-called purity of philosophy by isolating it from everyday affairs and ordinary experiences,[1] Rorty tirelessly undermined that essentialist or metaphysical thesis that informed their understanding of the tradition and discipline. To satisfy the demand of a postmodern culture and its readership, Rorty argues that in his *Philosophy and the Mirror of Nature*, philosophy is nothing but a form of conversation, held by and for those who have read and commented on the works by certain figures in the past; and it is indeed, a "conversation of mankind."

However, locating himself in a cross-cultural context, Rorty's position of anti-essentialism turned essentialist. Rorty seemed to suddenly decide to apply an a priori concept to philosophy in the presence of the comparative philosophers. He stated to his correspondent that philosophy is exclusively a Greek concept and practice and the modern institutionalization of this originally Greek intellectual form of inquiry is a Western practice. Therefore, those who practice philosophy in the academy are connected by an ancestral and genealogical linkage.[2]

For Balslev, Rorty's changing definition of philosophy is certainly an expression of ethnocentrism, or a form of philosophical essentialism. As she put it, with a sense of humor, Rorty has surely required a "birthright" of people who practice philosophy. She suspected the category of cultural Otherness may have informed Rorty's apparent inconsistency. Should Rorty be willing to reflect the self-understanding of philosophy in relation to the category of the Other and join the current, ongoing discussions on the "theme of cultural otherness," carried on in the other disciplinary studies such as anthropology, cultural studies and post-colonial studies, he may be able to see his own self-conflicting position and hence free himself from the essentialist thinking of the discipline of philosophy that has prevented him from participating in otherwise fruitful dialogue with his Eastern colleagues.

Rorty declined Balslev's invitation and simply stated that he found the very term "Otherness" "baffling."[3] As a good pragmatist, he could only see the category as a disguised philosophical term; and discussion of it could only suggest some unresolved social and political problems. If Balslev were to insist, they could perhaps talk about the specific categories of the Other, such as women, the weak and oppressed, or, the exotic. In the case of the former, one may get to know how social progress had improved the situation of women and the poor; and in the latter, one gets to appreciate how the romantic love of the exotic had inspired the imagination and sustained the rigor of European high culture. Balslev did not agree with Rorty's equation of the category of the Other with such social categories, and especially that of the exotic. For what Rorty referred to as the most creative expression of European high culture, the love of the exotic, has betrayed a Western sense of cultural superiority over the Other; and any imagination about the Other without serious learning about and adequate knowledge of it could only be a superficial practice.

We shall take a close look at the ways in which Rorty and Balslev debated their respective viewpoints while trying to determine what has prevented them from achieving a shared understanding of the aforementioned issues. In highlighting the overlooked and perhaps intentionally obscured areas such as the personal and cultural backgrounds that informed their respective positions and the proper cultural and academic contexts that shaped their viewpoints, we may help to reveal a hidden history of philosophy and its relationship to the category of the Other.

Is Philosophy the "conversation of mankind" or the "conversation of Europe"? Rorty's Problematic

During the correspondence, Balslev tried to clarify with Rorty about his latest view on philosophy by asking if he still held his earlier view about philosophy as a genre of writing—a body of commentary literature composed by those who can read and talk about certain philosophical figures such as "Plato, Newton, Kant, Marx, Darwin, Freud, Dewey, etc."[4] Should such be the case, the restriction of the practice of philosophy to the "family members," as Rorty specified in one of his letters to her, would be self-contradictory. Rorty's immediate reply to her question was rather straightforward: No, philosophy is not a genre of writing. Earlier, he made the mistake of defining philosophy as "a literary genre" and as a "format." Nor would it be a generic concept, if it were to be taken as an "instance of the concept to be established without reference to historical or cultural context."[5] Rorty explains, unlike the visual arts and musical notes, which could perhaps be organized interculturally and transhistorically, the written texts of philosophy have to be classified according to their respective histories and cultures.[6] As such, Rorty now tells Balslev, it is best to view it as a "tradition." As a tradition, Rorty further specified, philosophy is simply "a genealogical linkage connecting certain past figures with certain present figures" and "a way of noting that there is an ancestral relation of overlapping fibers,"[7] and such fibers were made of "Father Parmenides, honest Uncle Kant, and bad brother Derrida."[8]

What puzzles Balslev is the apparent essentialism or ethnocentrism that Rorty was perpetuating here that he had championed to subvert elsewhere. For those who read Rorty's other writings may have also noticed the apparent inconsistency in his definition of philosophy. Certainly, the inconsistency does not appear to be the result of the imprecise use of language, but a deliberate effort to shift the ground where he used to stand while defining philosophy.

A close look at his writings published in the 1970s and 1980s may help to explain Rorty's shift of the positions. During that time period, Rorty had committed himself to develop a new narrative account of the history of philosophy, aiming to free the discipline from the essentialist self-understanding of its nature and social function. From 1979 to 1982, Rorty published two important collections of essays, *Philosophy and the Mirror of Nature* and *Consequences of Pragmatism*, in which Rorty tells stories about the history of philosophy to different audiences at different occasions. In his telling, philosophy was first perceived as "the love of wisdom" in Platonic fashion, and later as a "mere polemical device" utilized by the scholastic community to "exclude from the field of honor those whose pedigrees are unfamiliar." In the modern era, and especially in the modern Cartesian tradition, philosophy was expected "to uncover the grounds of knowledge," and a philosopher was to be the "epistemological police," safeguarding the truth. To liberate philosophy from all those classical and modern confinements, Rorty proposed, we need to reassign the role for philosophy and to transform it into a form of dialogue that cultivates "the ability to sustain a conversation."[9] To this end, the philosophers of the postmodern age should transform themselves into "cultural critics,"[10] who can charm "hermetic thinkers" out of their "self-enclosed practices" for a discussion or conversation.

Such a conversation is open to those who "have read and pondered Plato, Newton, Kant, Marx, Darwin, Freud, Dewey, etc." In essence, the noble aspiration of philosophy in the postmodern age is to sustain "a conversation of mankind."[11]

Yet Rorty modified his position by narrowing down the scope of the conversation in a context in which he had to address Jürgen Habermas's concern about the possible "ideological distortions" of such a conversation. For Habermas, there is always a need to specify the conditions of possibility for such a conversation, because there will always be ideological corruptions of "an ideal speech situation."[12] Rorty mocked Habermas for even having raised such a concern, which shows that Habermas had gone back to "the transcendental and offers principles."[13] Rorty's anti-essentialist position allowed him to see that the goal of the conversation cannot be determined in advance but only perceived during the course of it, "with regard to the concrete advantages or disadvantages of a given point of view" of the participants.[14] However, as one of his commentators observed, Rorty's philosophical relativism turned into a radical ethnocentrism as he proceeded to discuss the need to assert certain values when conflicts arise with other conversation partners who are from non-European traditions. According to Rorty, if there are indeed any rules that are considered to be virtuous and useful, they have to come from whatever emerges from the conversation of Europe. That is, in order to have an "undistorted" conversation, if there were to be one, Rorty suggested that we—"the people who have read and pondered Plato, Newton, Kant, Marx, Darwin, Freud, Dewey, etc."[15]—have to "employ *our* criteria of relevance" to whatever situations that conversation finds itself in. Although, he could not justify "truth," "knowledge," and "morality" on a universal basis to the other conversation participants of non-European heritage, he would still have to assert the value of these terms by simply stating that they are developed with "the details of the culture" to which he belongs. Therefore, he has to take the notions of truth and virtue and whatever else from the conversation of Europe. If anybody wishes to raise questions about "what is so special about Europe" and Europeans, he or she would only be provided with an "irrational" answer, that is, we, the Europeans, are in a privileged position simply by *being us*.[16] Georgia Warnke, one of Rorty's critics, observed that Rorty's reasoning for shifting philosophy from "the conversation of mankind" to the "conversation of Europe" was a pure expression of "irrationalism."[17]

Indeed, Rorty admitted his ethnocentric position. For arguments about an undistorted conversation in line with Western values sanctified by the canonical philosophy that he and his fellow philosophers find important and significant is "frankly ethnocentric."[18] Yet, ethnocentrism is all he had; and if anyone was interested in challenging his position, he had to throw the question back at him or her by asking, "Do you have anything non-European to suggest which meets our European purpose better?"[19]

Rorty's assertions of his privileged status of being himself resonate with various ethical, cultural, or political fundamentalist claims about the superiority of a certain ethnic origin, of a specific cultural tradition or political ideology as the very ground for excluding and rejecting other groups of peoples without being able to offer any rational justification. Warnke pointed out that "to concede a frank ethnocentrism" could only mean one thing with Rorty, that is, the philosophical conversation that he had advocated earlier is not "open to all on an equal basis." If the terms of condition for the conversation have to come from the conversation of Europeans, there would be no access for the non-Europeans to participate in philosophy. In Rorty's words, Warnke quoted, "we Western liberal intellectuals should accept the fact that we have to start from where we are, and that means that there are views which simply cannot be taken seriously."[20] Consequently, as Warnke observed, with Rorty, the conversation of mankind cannot substitute for the idea of Reason, since there is no way to justify the West's commitment to such a rational conversation; and "commitment is simply part of the conversation of the West as we Westerners understand it."[21]

It seems, according to Warnke , the only effective way to converse with Rorty is to become irrational like Rorty himself. One could only throw Rorty's questions back at him by asking why he is more "frankly *ethnocentric* than frankly *ethnophobic*." Why did he stick with the European tradition and "the conversation of Europe" for no better reasons than simply because they are, his own? Instead of praising virtues such as truth-seeking and morality-driving, why did he also include the names such as Hitler and Stalin into the conversation of Europe?[22]

Philosophy and the "Theme of Otherness"—a Cultural Critique Offered by Balslev and Others

In Balslev's viewpoint, Rorty's irrationalism and ethnocentric position on philosophy is by no means an isolated instance, but typify an intricate connection between the question of the Other and the production of ideas in the Western academy of philosophy. For Balslev, the problem of the Other is one of the most ancient themes that has preoccupied the Western mind ever since the very conception of philosophy; and the problems of the "one and the many, identity and difference, are ancient themes of philosophy."[23] The questions whether there is philosophy in Asia and whether "Asians need philosophy the way that the Europeans did," as Rorty asked, were not mere "cultural accidents," but a reflection of the long-standing practice that had perpetuated the category of Otherness and hence a Eurocentric view of philosophy, which sees that "there is not in the East any project of thinking at all like that of Greek *philosophia*."[24]

In one of her letters Balslev related to Rorty, recently, that a seminar on philosophy and cultural Otherness was held at the Commonwealth Center at the University of Virginia. The participants collectively testified that the notion of the Other is "a recurrent topic for debates and discussion of our time," and that the "theme of otherness is virtually appearing in a wide range of disciplinary studies," whether it was implicitly assumed or actively engaged. For Balslev, the current interest in addressing "what constitutes the Other" in the disciplinary studies provided a good opportunity for philosophers to "explore the otherness in an authentic manner, taking note of its cross-cultural dimension."[25] To get Rorty involved in such an effort would perhaps enable him to gain a better self-understanding of his ethnocentrism and the apparent inconsistency in defining what philosophy should be. In addition, Balslev speculated, Rorty may be able to shed some light on how the category of the Other had been conceived, developed, and articulated in the Western history of ideas and the academy of philosophy.

Balslev's serious interest in engaging the question of Otherness and the cross-cultural dimension of philosophy is consistent. A few years after the Hawaii conference, which had served as a platform of exchange with Rorty, she edited and published a collection of critical essays contributed to by visiting scholars at the Center for Cultural Research at Arrhus University in Denmark in 1994, entitled *Cross-Cultural Conversation*. In the Introduction, she wrote that in recent years the category of the Other has translated itself into the notion of a "boundary." In a positive and "a soft sense," boundary "speaks of a plurality of cultures," and encourages the discussion of "the inner divergence" and "tensions within" one cultural system. In a negative and "a strong sense," boundary "signifies a barrier or a hindrance" that prohibits "crossing," and treats crossing as "trespassing."[26] It is this hard and inflexible sense of boundary that "obstructs the perceptions of the overlapping contents" of "the destinies of traditions and cultures" that she wished to explore. Her questions for Rorty are thus: Is comparative philosophy an institutional Other to the establishment of philosophy that it trespasses? Are comparative philosophers, who choose to engage the other intellectual traditions, trespassers? If the cultural, linguistic, and intellectual boundaries do not permit any crossing, should we just accept the old cliché that we all live in different conceptual worlds and that we are all the pensioners of our respective languages?

Before discussing Rorty's response to Balslev's questions, it may be helpful to locate the theme of cultural Otherness that Balslev had identified in a historical and theoretical context. This will enable us to determine the legitimacy of Balslev's claim that there had been a causal connection between philosophy and the theme of cultural Otherness and that the West's coping with it remains philosophically ambiguous.

Lars-Henrik Schmidt, a contributor to *Cross-Cultural Conversation*, pointed out that the category of the Other has always occupied center stage in the development of ideas and philosophical traditions. There has existed a causal connection between the historical treatment of and the contemporary discussion of cultural Otherness; and the latter is the "continuation of the three grand Western traditions of Christianity, Humanism, and the Enlightenment."[27] He gave a good historical survey of how these three grand Western intellectual traditions attempted to treat the Otherness of the Other and how the category had undergone a systematic change. At the beginning, Schmidt stated, the notion of the Other originated with the "idea of human dependence, of the lack of independence (sameness) and the subsequent striving for this very independence (sameness)."[28] According to Schmidt, the realization of human finitude projects itself into a relation with the Other—the otherness of nature, of fellow human beings, and of oneself. For instance, in classical Christian thought, "the other is considered to be the absolute other; that is to say God or nature." The Other as God or nature is an exterior Other who has the authority to render humans "humane," yet remains outside and above the human realm and humanity. With the emergence of humanism, which to a great degree sprang from the Christian tradition, divine Otherness became internalized, which may not be comprehended but can surely be experienced in one's relations with one's neighbors, or fellow human beings, through the figure of Jesus Christ. Schmidt tells, by the age of enlightenment, the category of the Other translates itself, this time, into "something to be experienced in one's own being."[29] The Otherness is our very '*Menschlichkeit*,'" as Kant put it; or it is "a '*homme en general*' participating in us but which is not identical to us," as Rousseau tells. By the age of enlightenment and in the development of modern philosophy, the Other had assumed a dual status, as Schmidt pointed out. On the one hand, it stands for a transcendental principle, (i.e., "humanity as such"), and on the other, a concrete historical moment that gives the individual a personal identity.[30]

However, we may add that the Western treatment of the Other went well beyond the grand traditions of Christianity, Humanism, and the age of enlightenment and reached its completion with Hegel's development of dialectics in the nineteenth century. Most importantly, Hegel's dialectics seemed to have successfully translated and transcribed the cultural Other, through the comparison of the Greek culture with that of the non-Greek, into a discipline boundary—the boundary that discriminates the unique history of Western philosophy from all the non-Western intellectual traditions.

We shall take a moment to briefly examine how Hegel had accomplished such a task. One recalls, in his lectures on the *Vorlesungen uber philosophie der Weltgeschichte* that Hegel delivered in Berlin from 1822 to 1831, he set a standard framework to identify and subsequently exclude the cultural Other from the paradigm of world history and world philosophy. Hegel's discussion of the characteristics of the land of Africa exemplifies his strategy of identifying and excluding the non-Greek cultural Other. According to Hegel, Africa was an "unhistorical continent, with no movement or development of its own." Except for North Africa and Egypt, which were "orientated towards Europe," the continent was inhabited by a population who had not reached "an awareness of any substantial objectivity—for example, of God or Law"—in which man could participate in and become aware of his own being. Such a lack of substantial objectivity creates an "undifferentiated and concentrated" stage in which the African man failed to separate himself from "an absolute being which is other and higher than him," and to make "distinction between himself as an individual and his essential universality."[31]

Thus, with reference to the Greeks and their cultural and religious development in the Mediterranean world, Hegel clearly laid out not only the distinctively *cultural* but also *intellectual* differences between the Mediterranean world and the African continent, and for that matter, the differences between Europe and Asia. The lack of objective awareness of a transcendental being yields to an incapability of discriminating oneself not only from the absolute Other—God or Law—but also from the universal humanity from which one derives one's nature of being human. Such a lack of discriminating capability, and thus the entanglement with the undifferentiated cosmic whole in the histories of African and Asian cultures, betrays an absence of a self-transcending Spirit that is the prerequisite of the dialectical fulfillment of world history and world philosophy.

Hegel's thesis was expanded and elaborated by his contemporaries and later historians of ideas as well, who further perpetuated the cultural and intellectual differences between the European and non-European peoples. In an influential work, *Geschichte der Philosophie* by Wilhelm Windelband, published in 1892, we find that Hegel's notion of the self-consciousness and self-transcendence of European thought suddenly gained a "scientific" nature. The perceived scientific nature of its philosophy, as Windelband specified, reflected in the "the work of intelligence which seeks knowledge methodically for its own sake." Such a scientific spirit only evolved with "the Greek of the sixth century BC," which found no parallel in its contemporary cultures in China and India. Unlike that of the Greeks, the intellectual activities of the Chinese and Indians were driven by mere "practical needs," or "mystical fancy," and to these ends, they either compiled an "abundance of information on single subjects" or offered generalized "views of the universe."[32] The self-understanding of the scientific nature of its philosophical system was thus established through the comparison with its cultural Other—the non-Western world. The framework of philosophy's self-understanding by Hegel and Windelband remained largely unchallenged in the twentieth century. The subsequent philosophers continued to echo with Hegel and Windelband. For instance, Edmund Husserl, in his *Philosophy and the Crisis of Humanities*, strongly objected to locating Chinese and Indian philosophy on the same "plane" with that of Greek philosophy, and states that one should not be blind to "the most essential difference of principle" in the intellectual systems between the West and the East. Whereas the thinkers in India and China were searching for knowledge in the attempt to fulfill "a vocation-like, life-interest," the Greek thinkers looked for "the essentially new form of a purely 'theoretical' attitude, merely motivated by '*theoria*,' and nothing but *theoria*."[33]

More recently, there are voices contesting Western philosophy's self-understanding sanctified by its canonical thinkers. Philosophy was not always born from "the love of wisdom" and motivated by a "pure understanding" of the nature of the world in mathematical entities and abstract principles; nor has the search for knowledge been merely orientated for the sake of knowledge alone. Don Howard, professor of philosophy, reminded us that in the modern history of philosophy, there were different stories told at different points of time about what philosophy was; and different justifications for the need to philosophize, which did not always happen to "correspond to a timeless Platonic form,"[34] sustained by a pure theoretical interest, independent from life interest and vocational necessity. For example, the Enlightenment's distinction between philosophy and religion, and the subsequent separation of philosophy from theology, and the institutionalization of philosophy into an academic program in the modern German state were all done "for a purpose," a purpose other than the "love of wisdom" or the passion to understand abstract principles.[35] The practical need then, Howard reminded us, was to develop a new discipline in the universities to "train young men for careers in civil administration in service to a state that is to become a center of power distinct from the church."[36]

However, in his *Desire, Dialectics and Otherness*, William Desmond observed that there is a change of trend in the academy of philosophy in the postmodern West. Contrary to conventional philosophy's exclusive attitude towards its cultural Other, that of the non-Greek traditions, the postmodern philosophers seemed to display an intense interest in cultural Otherness as a philosophical category. Postmodern thinkers, from Nietzsche, Heidegger, Foucault, and Derrida, all seem to have explored the "desire and elusive recesses beyond the threshold of self-possessed consciousness," which has initiated a move into "realms of otherness" to form a resistance to Hegelian "philosophical dialectics." There are explanations for this seemingly strange turn of the postmodern philosophy, according to Desmond. That is, though the modern West has comfortably settled down with the notion of dialectical totality and accepted Hegel's determination of the "sameness over otherness, identity over difference, and unity over plurality,"[37] yet it also recognizes that Hegel's dialectical totality has exhausted itself as a philosophical system to accommodate future change. The anxiety of this perceived self-exhaustion has since promoted the postmodern celebration of the Other, or the Otherness of the Other, among other things, as a way to reopen its closed up system in order to cope with the new social and cultural dynamics.

Schmidt would have agreed with Desmond's observation. He also observed that postmodernism has indeed transformed the dual status of the Other—the transcendental and historical, assumed by the Enlightenment. This transformation resulted in, on the one hand, man's "unconscious structure" manifested in psychological, linguistic, and kinship structures as analyzed by Foucault in his *The Order of Things*; and on the other, the "cultural differences" of the non-Western societies to be experienced and studied by social scientists. Thus, the category of cultural Other once more became significant.[38] However, we may point out, for some scholars of the post-colonial studies, the postmodern philosophical celebration of the cultural Other to revolt against Hegelian dialectics may further perpetuate the marginalization of the category of the Other, which we shall soon discuss.

Rorty's Response to the Category of the Other—a Pragmatist Position

In spite of the awareness of the various discourses on the category of the Other, Rorty chose to deny its legitimacy and its perceived philosophical significance. From a pragmatist perspective, Rorty simply stated, the question of the Other and any related categories such as "one and many, of identity and difference," are all "artificial" constructs.[39] If they are perceived as significant, it is because they are reviewed from "a doctrine of real essence" and something that cannot be coped with in a practical manner. The slogan of a pragmatist is thus: "all philosophical problems are disguised problems," if the Other does not make "a difference to what we do, it makes no difference at all."[40]

Rorty warned that there may always be an alluring metaphysical temptation at the backs of our minds when discussing the category of the Other. We need to watch out for the tendency to equate it with that of the unknown, such as God; an abstract form or "the inside" experiences of another human being.[41] For a good pragmatist, there is no experience that can not be articulated in language or mediated in a linguistic event. Invoking Davidson's claims that there is no such a thing as "an unlearnable language," and that the possibility of being bilingual is always open, Rorty thus argued that any experience of the Other, without exception, is linguistically accessible. Similar to the learning of a foreign language, the understanding of the "strangeness" or the Otherness of the Other is to "figure out why the other is saying the strange things he or she does."[42] Realizing any human experiences are linguistically accessible and that language is no more than a useful tool to "cope with different problems" presented by our natural and social environment, we can certainly gain access to the experience of the Other, Rorty assured us. Different cultures or groups use different languages to cope with the natural, social, and environmental problems, which may erect barriers for cross-cultural understanding, yet, as long as the possibility of learning of the other languages exists and the opportunity of "bilingualism is always open,"[43] as Rorty sees it, the problem of cultural otherness is dissolved.

It is interesting to note here that Rorty did not seem to realize how his linguistic solutions to problems of the Other contradicted his previous position on the exclusive nature of philosophy. For if the understanding of the Other can be equated with the acquisition of a foreign language, his claim that philosophy in the West is a genealogy that is only accessible by its family members cannot be valid. We may argue that if the knowledge and experience of the cultural Other is attainable, analogous to that of learning a foreign language, a cross-cultural understanding of philosophy should also be achievable.

Rorty's turn to a linguistic idealism raises some other issues as well. Given the alleged transparent relation between language, consciousness, and perceived reality that has been challenged by various disciplinary studies since the time of Nietzsche, it is not unproblematic now for anyone to claim the correspondence between these three categories. Further, Rorty's pragmatist reduction of the category of the Other into a linguistic event, and for that matter, the unknown into the realm of the empirical, could be very limiting in the exploration and understanding of the world, both immediate and mediated. For such a reductionism conveniently takes out any experiences that are not immediately transparent to language or measurable by empirical means, and it suppresses any spiritual, religious, or psychological exploration of the world, which had inspired so many discoveries and creative expressions. Further, we may argue, if the understanding of the Other is reducible to the matter of coping with the technical inconvenience of learning a foreign language, what we have by now would be one standardized version of world history, transparent and accessible to all cultures and societies.

Now we may go back to how Rorty further argued with Balslev about the perceived problem of the Other. He explicitly suggested that if Balslev still insists on discussing the category of the Other as a philosophical problem, she should at least translate it into some concrete social categories. For instance, she may think of the Other as women, the poor and weak, or the foreign and exotic. Such a translation would allow the understanding of the Other in more concrete and realistic terms. For example, let us think of women as the Other to men, in a male-dominated history and society. In Rorty's view, feminist philosophers were somewhat successful in asserting rights for women and improving women's social and economic status. Yet, this success was not due to feminist discourses on the ultimate unknown—the so-called women's experiences in a kind of "pre-linguistic state called 'feminine,'" but rather due to the ways in which feminists provided society with a vivid narrative account of women's suffering as social beings in patriarchal societies.[44] As far as the Other as the weak and poor are concerned, Rorty frankly admitted that he had very little to relate to these groups of peoples as a professor living in the richest part of the world. He understood that these categories of peoples have perhaps very minimal means of existence, and were constantly subjected to oppression and brutality. However, the only effective way to release them from such terrible conditions perpetuated by their own histories and cultures is to increase the accumulation of social wealth and change the means of distributing money and power. Again, to accomplish such objectives, Rorty once again pointed toward the Western model of modernization—liberal democracy, science, technology and so on.[45]

Rorty finally suggested to Balslev that they discuss the category of the Other in the context of the nineteenth century European Romanticists' "love of the exotic." For Rorty, the Romanticists developed a love and taste for the foreign and exotic, and used it to appropriate a radically different way of speaking and acting for themselves. In this context, the Romanticists were not afraid of losing their identities, but rather strove to get rid of them. For the search for radically different styles, ways of speaking, and acting had driven the Romanticist to enlarge his or her "imagination" and eventually realize "a larger, freer self."[46] Thus it is this Romanticist love of the exotic that had sustained and enriched the vitality of the European high culture; and it is this kind of love that "has become an important feature" and a "progressive element" of Western civilization.[47] Rorty shifted the focus of cross-cultural encounter from *understanding of* the Other to the *use of* the Other for self-fulfillment, and in so doing disconnected himself from a critical post-colonial position that reinstated the suffering inflicted on the colonial objects by the arbitrary and often manipulative representation of the colonial subject. In spite of his awareness of Edward Said's critical assessment of Western Orientalist literature, Rorty chose to ignore, in Said's words, "the unspoken strategy" in the treatment of Europe's Other by the colonial subjects.

A Post-Colonial Critique of the Love of the Exotic

Rorty's praise of the Romantic love of the exotic poses some serious problems for Balslev, and perhaps, for those who are sympathetic readers of post-colonial literature as well. From Balslev's perspective, the use of the exotic, that was embodied in foreign symbols and imageries from a foreign land, for the sole purpose of enriching the self-expression and new identity, is dangerously "superficial"—to say the least.[48] Rorty's remarks about the power of imagination and creativity of the European Romanticists could actually yield to a distorted understanding of the cultural and spiritual value embodied in those foreign objects and images. Balslev thus suggested that it is always necessary to make serious efforts to learn about the hard facts and information of what appeared to be the exotic from other cultures before freely exercising one's imagination. This process of getting the hard facts and information about the other traditions is not be so different from the education process that Rorty advocated elsewhere. Balslev reminded him that he had stated, in his paper "Education, Socialization, and Individualization," the same year he spoke at the East-West philosophy conference in Hawaii, that education cannot "encourage imagination without a preparation of memorized information, or encourage individual talent without imparting a shared tradition."[49] Putting Rorty's remarks into a cross-cultural context, Balslev once again pointed out Rorty's inconsistancy in dealing with similar issues.

As we are aware of Balslev's protest against Rorty's praise of the Romantic love of the exotic is not an isolated instance in contemporary post-colonial studies. There is indeed an increasing critical awareness of the troublesome nature of representing the foreign, the native, and the exotic. In fact, it is the post-colonial literature and critiques of the colonial representation of colonized peoples and cultures as the ultimate Other that had shaped Balslev's critical sensibility.

The gaining of independence of Arabic, African, Indian, and South Asian nations from the colonial yoke of the Western Empire in the 1950s is also accompanied by the outcry for autonomy from the cultural hegemony of the Empire. The possibility to create an independent cultural identity undermines the colonial paradigm of knowledge and representation of the natives as the Other—the Other as a speechless and motionless object, exited only for the display under a colonial gaze. A systematic critical assessment of the cultural domination of the Empire was perhaps developed from Said's work on *Orientalism*, published in 1978. Said analyzed the ways in which not only the Western political and economic power subjugated colonized peoples, but how the Western paradigms of knowledge, such as Hegelian dialectics and its modes of representation, had effectively suppressed and silenced the self-expression of non-Western peoples and cultures. The native or the cultural Other, for instance, the Islamic East, was either neutralized or absorbed by a representing colonial subject, and hence lost its radical Otherness and differences. This gesture of neutralizing the radically different cultural Other, in Said's opinion, enabled the colonial subject to rationalize and objectify the cultural experiences and historical voices of the natives. Anthropologist James Clifford agreed with Said's critique. He also pointed out that the reduction of the natives into "static images" had caused major devastating consequences, among which, the concrete human experiences of the other cultures were objectified into "an asserted authority on one side and a generalization on the other."[50] In spite of some theoretical difficulties inherent in the critique of Western Orientalism, Said's and Clifford's call for the indigenous intellectuals, the natives, as well as the self-critical Western liberal thinkers to "write back" at the colonial Empire was actively received. The body of critical literature generated in recent decades formed "a new multivocal field of intercultural discourse" that bravely challenged "the Western gaze."[51] Clifford commented, for centuries the West had studied and spoken for the rest of the world, now the "objects" for study and observation began to "write back."[52]

Within the framework set up by Said and Clifford, some postcolonial writers decided to explore the topic of love of the exotic in the postmodern context. In her *Writing Diaspora*, Rey Chow discussed the problematic entailed in the current interest in deconstructing the colonial representation of the native as a silent image and a motionless object. Chow pointed out that the decent intention of "restoring the native to its original context" and to right the wrongs may further perpetuate the colonial legacy and hence exploit the native one more time. The instance in her mind was a piece of writing by a post-colonial writer who claimed to be able to decolonize "a European phantasm," represented in a postcard made of the images of Algerian women by a French photographer during colonial times by returning this "postcard to its sender." Chow finds the author's claim to be very problematic. For one way to send the postcard back to the sender is to "fill in the space left open by the silent women"; and yet, the open space is the very witness to the otherwise original account of the suffering these women endured in the process of being reduced to visual objects and then put on exhibition. Should such a space be filled up, the opportunity to witness and tell will be permanently lost. For Chow, the author's position is not essentially different than that of the visible French colonial photographer, for both of them have projected their gaze "over the images of these women," who become the "bearers of multiple exploitation."[53]

Chow thus warned that the age of the post-colonial and postmodern is "the age of discursive reproduction," in which it is the natives who are likely to become victimized again. Unlike the representation of colonized objects, the discursive production is engendered by the distinctly different and yet interrelated processes of double displacement: first, the "commoditization by diversion" and second, "the aesthetics of decontextualization."[54] Chow quoted Arjun Appadurai, another postcolonial writer, in this description of double displacement:

> Value...is accelerated or enhanced by placing objects and things in unlikely context.... This enhancement of value through the diversion of commodities from their customary circuits underlies the plunder of enemy valuables in warfare, the purchase and display of "primitive" utilitarian objects, the framing of "found" objects, the making of collections of any sort. In all these examples, diversions of things combine the aesthetic impulse..., and the touch of the morally shocking.[55]

Is there any way left to encounter the native without the images? Could "a correct" image of the ethnic specimen substitute for an "incorrect" one? Or could one give the native "voice" behind "her 'false' image"? In Chow's opinion, the answers are no. Chow finds herself in agreement with Derrida's commentator, Gayatri Spivak, who had once stated that "if the subaltern can speak then, thank God, the subaltern is not a subaltern anymore."[56] For speaking itself "belongs to an already well-defined structure and history of domination."[57] Thus for both Spivak and Chow, not only are there no discursive ways—verbal or visual—available for the non-natives to encounter or see the natives, but there are no available means for the natives to speak or represent themselves either, since any verbal and visual devices are part and parcel of the intellectual device of the Empire. In fact, the most effective strategy for natives to resist second-time victimization is to remain silent;

and non-natives to help the natives to retain or restore the originally lost silence. By making a choice not to speak, natives are effectively expressing voiceless resistance that may stop any further perpetuation of colonial legacy. Such a silence would then become a powerful indicator of "the inaccessibility of, or un-translatability from one mode of discourse in a dispute to another"—namely, from the subaltern discourse into the imperialist one.[58]

Said also commented on the dilemma of encountering the natives as the Other. A decade after the publication of his *Orientalism*, Said seemed to reach a rather pessimistic conclusion. That is, the battle against the Western modes of representation of the Oriental Other seems to be doomed to failure. Take modern anthropology's creation of a native "interlocutor," for example. In his essay "Representing the Colonized," published in *Critical Inquiry* in 1989, Said discussed ways how an "interlocutor" was identified for the dialogue with anthropologists from the West. First of all, it is within a highly controlled environment that an interlocutor was carefully identified and chosen. He was brought in "scrubbed, disinfected," and "disarmed of the guns and stones at the doorstep," and "checked in with the porter." Such a creature betrays, Said lamented, "The urgent situation of crisis and conflict that brought him or her in the first place."[59] Further, the falsification of such a lab interlocutor best exemplifies not only a "political economy" in the post-colonial reproduction of the inferiority of the non-European cultural Others, but the social and cultural situation that makes its discourse "both so possible and so sustainable." For, to have a dialogue with the native is to fulfill the "fashionable theoretical correlatives" (i.e., Habermas's "ideal speech situation" or Rorty's "philosophical conversation"), since all of these instances require an interlocutor. Hence, Said realized that his critiques of the Western representation of its cultural Other could only be a "negative polemic which does not advance a new epistemological approach or method," but only expresses a "desperation at the impossibility of ever dealing seriously with other cultures."[60]

Could it ever be possible to go around Said's negative polemic, Chow's silent resistance, and Rorty's pragmatist reduction of the category of the Other? Are there any constructive ways to formulate the question of cultural Otherness in relation to the discourse of philosophy or the intellectual enquiry of the ultimate questions underlining human existence? With these questions, we now turn to another instance of a cross-cultural encounter—a conversation between Martin Heidegger and his Japanese visitor.

PART III.
MARTIN HEIDEGGER'S
DIALOGUE WITH
A JAPANESE
VISITOR

Chapter 3

ON THE WAY TO A "COMMON" LANGUAGE

> Language is the flower of the mouth. In language,
> the earth blooms towards the blooms of the sky.
> —Heidegger, "The Nature of Language"

> Language is the petals that stem from *Koto.*
> —Tezuka, the Japanese Visitor in Martin Heidegger's
> "The Dialogue on Language"

Heidegger is probably one of the few influential European thinkers of the twentieth century whose sustained interest in Eastern texts and thinkers is well recognized among comparative philosophers. In 1969, an international symposium was held at the East-West Center on the campus of the University of Hawaii to honor Heidegger's eightieth birthday, celebrating his relationship and dialogue with the Eastern world. In the letter addressed to the conference organizers, Heidegger stated: "again and again, it had seemed urgent to me that a dialogue take place with the thinkers of what is to us the Eastern world."[1]

According to the recollections of his students and commentators, while still drafting *Being and Time* in the 1920s, Heidegger had already familiarized himself with the classical texts of Chinese Daoism and Japanese Zen Buddhism and established personal contacts with thinkers from the Far East. Heidegger held a series of conversations with the Japanese scholars and students, collaborated with a Chinese scholar in translating the Daoist texts into the German language, and was interviewed on television with a Buddhist monk.[2] His reading knowledge of Zen Buddhist and Daoist texts and working experiences with Eastern thinkers have exercised a certain degree of influence on his thinking and philosophical vocabularies.[3] Conversely, Heidegger's call for a "plenary thinking" by attempting to overcome the conventional metaphysical segregation of Being from beings had drawn serious responses from thinkers from the Eastern world. East-West comparative scholarship on Heidegger reached its maturity when another international conference was held eighteen years later on the same site of the University of Hawaii campus. The conference papers published under the title *Heidegger and Asian Thought*, were dedicated to Heidegger's aspiration to reach for a meaningful East-West dialogue, as well as to his expressed doubts for such a cross-cultural venture. Professor Graham Parkes, the editor of the anthology, once again reminded us of Heidegger's saying, that is, "these doubts hold equally true for both European and East Asian language, and above all for the realm of their possible dialogue." Neither side can by itself open and establish this realm.[4]

This chapter will focus on Heidegger's dialogue with a Japanese visitor, Professor Tezuka from the Imperial University, Kyoto. "A Dialogue on Language" was later published along with Heidegger's other language lectures under the title *Unterwegs zur Sprache* in 1959, and its English translation, *On the Way to Language,* became available in 1971. The Dialogue addresses three independent but interrelated issues that shed some new light on what we discussed in previous chapters regarding the nature of cross-cultural understanding and the legitimacy of East-West comparison. The first issue discussed is the nature of human language. In Heidegger's view, language is not merely linguistic signs employed in daily communication but "the house of Being"—an ontological construct that claims the being of its residents as they speak its tongue. The issue that the Dialogue needs to resolve first is whether, similar to what Rorty and Balslev disputed about the origin of philosophy in their correspondence, there could be a "common" language that enables Germans and Japanese (or Heidegger and Tezuka) to understand each other? Second, since Heidegger argued that hermeneutics was not merely a "methodology of interpretation," supposedly to guarantee a universal access to the meaning of the written texts, but rather, a way of being-in-the-world by listening and retrieving the "message" of one's own "destiny," could Germans and Japanese be able to articulate to one another the messages granted to them through there respective traditions? Third, in Heidegger's appropriation, the notion "hermeneutic relation" was not to be understood in terms of a market type of "demand

and supply" characterized by a mutual reciprocity. Could an actual cross-cultural encounter, such as the meeting between Heidegger and the Japanese visitor constitute a hermeneutic relationship?

The present chapter will only discuss the first issue that the Dialogue addresses, that of the nature of language (leaving the two other issues, hermeneutics and hermeneutic relationship for treatment in the next chapter). Heidegger's thinking and reflection on the nature of human language evolved and changed from the time he drafted *Being and Time* in the 1920s to the time he delivered his series of language lectures in the 1950s. The present study will demonstrate that such a change is traceable as he moved beyond the confinement of his native traditions, Greek and Germanic, to engage the cosmic thinking of the origin of language in the East Asian tradition, as witnessed in the Dialogue. We will discuss how Heidegger managed to change his metaphors for language from "house of Being" to "Saying" and to "the flower of the mouth," which illustrate the cross-cultural dimension of his thought, developed through his interaction with Eastern texts and thinkers. Spelling out the cross-cultural dimension of Heidegger's thinking on language, we can supply not only a link between his early and later thought on the subject matter, which appears to be missing in present day Heideggarian scholarship, but also help to reveal a new mode of the East-West exchange and dialogue that is not preoccupied with a priori categories nor shaped by abstract principles, but a hermeneutic engagement with each other's traditions that gradually yields to a slow mutation of the thought process and occasions of mutual understanding on a particular issue.

The Meeting with the Visitor

The "Dialogue on Language" between Heidegger and Tezuka began with the recollection of Count Shuzo Kuki, a mutual acquaintance to both Heidegger and his current visitor. Count Kuki came to Europe on an eight-year study tour in the 1920s and worked with Bergson, Husserl, and later, Heidegger. After his European tour, Kuki went back to Japan to take a teaching post at the Imperial University in Kyoto and became one of the three founding members of the Kyoto School of Philosophy. This new philosophical school emerged as a response to the radical changes taking place within Japanese society as it moved from the traditional to modern. The agenda of the Kyoto School was twofold: first, it intended to introduce modern European intellectual trends and philosophical ideas to the Japanese reading public: and second, it aimed to reconstruct classical Japanese intellectual traditions with the help of conceptual frameworks and analytical language from the European philosophical systems. According to the current visitor, Kuki's study tour reflected such a twofold agenda. While studying with the leading Western thinkers in Europe, Kuki had intended to reconstruct classical Japanese poetics "with the help of European aesthetics."[5] In retrospect, the visitor commented that Kuki's cultural mission seemed to remain unfulfilled, because the Japanese word *iki*, a key term in Japanese traditional poetics and artistic expression, remained untranslated. However, Kuki's unfulfilled cultural mission did not discourage the second generation of Japanese students from returning to Germany, and to Heidegger.

Heidegger also recalled the instances he met with Kuki at his own house. On such occasions, Kuki usually "remained silent" and sometimes, "he brought his wife along, who then wore festive Japanese garments," Heidegger recalled. Kuki's silence and his wife's colorful Japanese garments "made the Eastasian world more luminously present, and the danger of our dialogues became more clearly visible." Whenever Kuki did try to explain the word *iki* to him. Heidegger frankly admitted to the current visitor that he felt "the spirit of Japanese language remained closed—as it is to this day."[6] Now, the dilemma Heidegger presented to Tezuka was whether "it is necessary and rightful for Eastasians to chase after the European conceptual systems."[7]

The visitor, Tezuka, fully understood Heidegger's skepticism about a fruitful cross-cultural exchange and the problematic of translation described by Heidegger. He recalled that that in postwar Japan, while intellectuals still found Western metaphysical categories appealing, and the advent of technology inevitable, yet, they were also troubled by the fact that Western metaphysical and technological thought had not taken root in Japanese soil—in relation to the Japanese way of life and hence appeared to be "superficial."

Despite of the difficulties and challenges that had underlined previous interactions and exchanges, both Heidegger and Tezuka were interested in pursuing a dialogue. Without specific topics in their minds, the very issue of language came to the forefront. Drawing from his teacher's experiences, Tezuka pointed out that to use the modern German as a "common" language to converse on a culturally and linguistically Japanese topic, such as *iki*, may distort the content of the conversation; and to discuss *iki* and Japanese artistic experiences and poetics by converting them into Western aesthetic categories may destroy "the possibility of saying what the dialogue was about."[8] The critical awareness of such problems underlies cross-cultural translation and communication indicates a methodological maturity that had not been explicitly discussed in the previous German-Japanese meetings.

Heidegger agreed with his visitor that there may indeed be a possible distortion of any cross-linguistic translation and cross-cultural dialogue that they need to watch out for. However, there is another level of danger that lies hidden in the veiled nature of language itself that may pose an even greater threat. He pointed out that in the West, the obscured nature of language is intimately associated with the question of Being. Thus, the purpose of dialogue was not only to explore the problematic of cross-cultural translation, but the nature of language itself, which, incidentally, became the focus of the dialogue that they were about to pursue.

Language as "the house of Being"—Heidegger's First Language Metaphor

Before examining how the theme of language was discussed and how it implicated the cross-cultural understanding in this dialogue instance, we need to take a look at Heidegger's initial position on language, first shaped in his *Being and Time* in the 1920s and then developed and refined in his later language lecture series in the 1950s. A brief detour will thus help us to understand how Heidegger's thinking on language was conceived, developed, and eventually shifted away from the mainstream of Western thinking on metaphysics and metalinguistics, as it encountered a non-Western language world.

We may recall that as early as the 1920s, Heidegger had perceived an urgency to conduct the study of language in conjunction with philosophy's research on the question of Being. In his *Being and Time*, Heidegger called for such research and posed some primary questions for reflection on the subject matter. First, philosophical research must seek to determine "what kind of being that goes with language." Was it an equipment kind of being, ready-at-hand and within-the-world, or does it have *Dasien* kind of Being? These self-posed questions later became the focus of Heidegger's own philosophical investigation. To a great extent, he had provided answers to his own questions in the subsequent writing of *Poetry, Language, and Thought*, "Letter on Humanism," and *On the Way to Language*. In "Letter on Humanism," Heidegger first employed a metaphor to describe the relation of language with Being and human beings, the speaking beings of language:

> Language is the house of Being in which man exists by dwelling, in that he belongs to the truth of Being, guarding it.[9]

Here, language is presented as a metaphor. The metaphorical expression conveys several levels of meaning. First of all, language is not devised and used by human beings as an instrument for everyday communication—it is not "equipment" kind of being, as Heidegger would say. Rather, it must be differentiated from what is commonly called "linguistic signs" – phonetic writing or scripts invented by human speakers for the purpose of communication. Second, man finds in language the proper abode of his being or existence. Language is the collective historical and linguistic dwelling that man resides within even before he learns to speak its tongue. The ontological status of language thus negates a common assumption that man possesses language as a tool at-hand. Heidegger later on explained the relation between language and its speaker in the following terms: "What we speak of, language, is always ahead of us. Our speaking merely follows language constantly. Thus we are continually lagging behind what we first ought to have overtaken and taken up in order to speak constantly."[10] Thus, according to Heidegger, even the most authentic speakers of the language—the thinkers and poets—could only be the "custodians," but not the architects or owners, of the house in which they reside—the house of Being.

In his language lectures, Heidegger retained that language metaphor and reemphasized the ontological primacy of language in relationship to its speaker. Heidegger again stressed that "if we are to think through the nature of language, language must first promise itself to us, or must already have done so."[11] Language is not what was invented by man but is what enables him to speak and hence to become a man. As such, Heidegger thus concludes, language must be a *Dasein* kind of Being that "grants presence" and that "makes manifest." Language as such—that grants presence and makes manifest—in Heidegger's words, "is not identical with the sum total of all the words printed in a dictionary; instead . . . language is as *Dasein* is . . . it exists."[12] Apparently, Heidegger's perception on language radically differs from that of modern linguistics, which Heidegger refers to as "metalinguistics." Metalinguistics turned the human language into a system of signs and objects for disciplinary study to be pursued by linguists. The objectification of human language makes possible the "thoroughgoing technicalization of all languages into the sole operative instrument of interplanetary information."[13]

Informed by Heidegger's emphases on the primacy of the ontological nature of human language and his criticism of the metalinguistics and technological treatment of the subject matter, we may be able to appreciate why he feels it necessary to retain and relocate the same language metaphor in a cross-cultural context. He stated to his visitor:

> Some time ago, I called language, clumsily enough, the house of Being. If man by virtue of his language dwells within the claim and call of Being, then we Europeans presumably dwell in an entirely different house than Eastasian man."[14]

Heidegger's reluctance to allow any meaningful exchange between the residents of different "houses of Being" has also become clear. We may suggest, for Heidegger, language is proper to man not simply because he possesses the property of language; but because it is through that property that he was granted a special access to Being. Being discloses itself through language to and in man. To refer to the fact that someone does not speak a certain language is to say that he does not have the access to a specific house of Being. Thus, language differences between Germans and Japanese are not mere linguistic or technical, which could be mediated by the mechanism of translation. Different language-speaking beings reside in different houses of Being—collective linguistic and historical dwellings—responding to different claims made to them through their respective languages. The question that Heidegger had for his visitor thus becomes, could Germans and Japanese speak and understand each other if they were claimed by, presumably, two sets of claims from two different houses of Being?

To address Heidegger's concern, it seems, we need to find out what claim European language has made to its speakers. In Heidegger's view, in the West, the claim or the message from the house of Being to its residents is most explicitly revealed in two primary instances: the metaphysics originated from the ancient Greek thinking of Being as a constant presence and the subsequent development of modern technology shaped by the metaphysical thinking of Being. Should metaphysics and technology be the most revealing instances of Being that have claimed the Western man since the conception of the Western thought, what would be the claim that the Eastern tradition speaks to the Eastern man through its language? Was it possible that there is a similar claim that revealed itself to both Western and Eastern man? If so, would it be possible that Heidegger and his visitor could articulate the claim to each other in the instance of current dialogue? With caution, Heidegger stated to his visitor that he was not sure at this point if what he was trying "to think as the being of language is also adequate to the nature of East Asian languages."[15] However, what he would like to find out in the future was that, if:

> ...a nature of language can reach the thinking experience, a nature would offer the assurance that European-Western saying and Eastasian saying will enter into dialogue such that in it there sings something that wells up from a single source.[16]

The follow-up question that Heidegger poses to his visitor is thus:

> Do you have in your language a word for what we call language? If not, how do you experience what with us is called language?[17]

Language as "the petals that stem from Koto"— a Japanese Word for Language

Heidegger's question introduced a long pause into the conversation. The visitor responded that there had never been anyone who had asked him such a question. However, he stated that he did not find Heidegger's language metaphor foreign to his native way of thinking and saying language; as a matter of fact, he even sensed "a kinship" between Heidegger's and the Japanese thinking of language as "the essential being" rather than mere linguistic signs.[18] Feeling curious, Heidegger was eager to find out what word the Japanese use to convey the essential being of language.

With some caution, Tezuka told Heidegger that in Japanese, the word for language is *koto ba*. Before proceeding to explain this compound word, he found it necessary to bring Heidegger's attention to a perceived difference between his native Japanese and European languages. The Japanese language was usually perceived as a pictography in contrast to the phonetic nature of European languages. For instance, one part of the word *ba* simply means "leaves" or "petals." "Thinking of cherry blossoms or plum blossoms," Tezuka tried to depict a mental image for a physical object that the word designates for Heidegger.[19] However, the other part of the word, *Koto,* cannot be related to an image or a physical object, nor does it allow itself to be conferred to a corresponding German word. It seems, the visitor suggested, *koto* could be rendered better in terms of Japanese artistic experiences and poetics. Thus it may be helpful to revisit the word *iki* and try to render the word *koto* in reference to *iki*. Apparently Heidegger was particularly receptive to the suggestion of rendering of *koto* in terms of poetics and poetic images. For him, poetry and poetic imageries are in the closest neighborhood with language and thinking. As he stated elsewhere:

> Singing and thinking are the stems, neighbor to poetry. They grow out of Being and reach into its truth. Their relationship makes think of what Holderlin sings of the trees of the woods: "And to each other they remain unknown, so long as they stand, the neighboring trunks."[20]

As previously mentioned, the word *iki* remained untranslated during the previous meeting of Heidegger and Kuki; this time, the visitor suggested that he should try to render the word, step-by-step, with footnoting. He first attempted to render *iki* as "the gracious," with a specification that "the gracious" is "not in the sense of a stimulus that enchants." Here, Tezuka both used the European category of grace to designate *iki* and at the same time disassociated the later from the usual implication of the former. Second, he rendered "the gracious" as "the breath of the stillness of luminous delight," and yet, that delight is not a sensual pleasure stimulated by the impression received from the physical objects—again, it does not directly correspond to a European aesthetic category. In fact, *iki* carries "nothing anywhere of stimulus and impression," because "there is nothing out there to stimulate the sensual delight," Tezuka summarized.[21] In contrast to the modern European aesthetics that organize artistic and poetic experiences in terms of "subject and object relation" and "stimulus and impression," *iki* rejects all the binary categorizations and remains in itself both the source and the expression of aesthetic delight and pleasure.

To orient Heidegger into this distinctively oriental and Japanese poetic world, the visitor finds it useful to remind him that once he had rendered the Greek word *charis* into "graciousness," in his "Poetically Man Dwells." Heidegger was glad to be reminded of the instance, stating it is indeed that the Greek word *charis* meaning graciousness "is itself poetical, is itself... makes poetry." As such, it also "brings forward and forth the world and things."[22] Thus reminded, Heidegger was able to see a parallel between the Greek word *charis* and the Japanese word *iki*, and even felt encouraged to spell out the further connection between the two. He stated to his visitor that if the word *iki* was what he had tried to say in "graciousness," both may work like a "hint . . . that beckons on, and beckons to and fro" and that "ensnares, carries away—into stillness." The hint, Tezuka added, should be a kind of "message of the veiling that opens up."[23] Thus, *iki* was finally rendered as "the breath of stillness that makes this beckoning stillness come into its own," which "is the reign under which that delight is made to come."[24] Heidegger concluded with delight, that "all presences" may come together in the moment of "grace" or *iki*—the making of poetry that brings forth and reveals the hitherto concealed world and entities in "pure delight of the beckoning stillness."[25] With a good understanding of *iki* being established with Heidegger, the visitor proceeded to render *koto*. In light of *iki*, *koto* was that which

> always also names that which (in the event of naming) gives delight, itself, that which uniquely in each unrepeatable moment comes to radiance in the fullness of its grace.[26]

Similar to *iki*—the pure aesthetic pleasure or delight in itself that "carries nothing anywhere of stimulus and impression," *koto* names, and in the event of naming, it gives aesthetic pleasure to what is named, simultaneously bringing itself to its full realization in each unique naming instance. Like *iki*, *koto* also conveys a meaning of "bringing forward and forth" what had previously been concealed. Without being alienated by such a parallel drawn between *iki*, *koto*, and grace, Heidegger actually felt encouraged to create a link between them. He suggested *koto* as naming could perhaps be rendered as "the appropriating occurrence of the lightening message of grace."[27] Appropriation is the English translation of the German word *Ereignis* that Heidegger uses frequently. It derives from the root *eigen*, "own proper," and the verb *ereigen*, "to appropriate."[28] Language as an appropriating occurrence or "event" thus suggests that it brings itself to its own being as it names or speaks. In a manner of speaking, it also "brings forward" the message of the hitherto concealed world in the moment of "grace," or "pure delight of beckoning stillness." "Beautifully said!" the visitor in turn praised Heidegger's ability to spell out the different levels of meaning the words *iki*, grace, and *koto* carry. Mutually encouraged, Heidegger and Tezuka worked together to reveal a cosmic dimension of language. That is, if language or naming is the "lightening message of the graciousness that brings forth," it is "holding sway over that which needs the shelter of all that flourishes and flowers."[29] Sensing it was the right timing to get a full rendering of the meaning of *koto ba*, Heidegger asked: "as the name for language, what does *Koto ba* say?" "The petals that stem from *Koto*," the visitor answered. "What a wondrous word," and it is "inexhaustible to our thinking," Heidegger exclaimed.[30]

We can see here, a fusion of conceptual horizon emerging in the Dialogue. The previous hesitation seems to have given away to a sense of mutual satisfaction, because a "common" origin or the essential nature of language is now being achieved. We may summarize this mutual understanding of the nature of human language as follows. First, in both German and Japanese language worlds, language is that which names and appropriates while giving aesthetic delight to what is named and appropriated. Second, in so doing, language brings forth and opens up what had been previously concealed by calling things, beings, and entities into unique forms of being present. Third, while retrieving what had previously been concealed, language also gives shelter to all "living organism" that flourish and flower on the earth. And last, unlike Heidegger's previous metaphor, language is no longer an ontological construct that merely confines its speakers, but a cosmic event that holds sway over the world as it names and speaks and shelters all who reside on the earth and under the sky—all that is flourishing and flowering.

The manner in which the mutual understanding on the theme of language between Heidegger and Tezuka was achieved deserves a note here. We may notice that this mutual understanding emerges gradually as the conversation slowly progresses. There seemed to be no preoccupations on either side to push a certain agenda or to win an argument. Instead, both Heidegger and Tezuka are trying to proceed with caution from topics and issues that they are not familiar with, allowing themselves to be "awkward" inquirers, moving slowly toward what the one tries to say to the other, for "slowness rests upon shy reverence"—a moral virtue recommended by Heidegger in conducting thinking and dialogue. Such a moral virtue allows the parties involved to listen to what appears to be foreign and strange that one tires of explaining to the other, encouraging one to retrieve what would otherwise be overlooked or forgotten in one's own tradition only to discover what appeared to be foreign is actually already embedded as familiar in one's own tradition (we shall discuss this seemingly strange relation of foreign and familiar in the last chapter). For instance, Heidegger's departure from the Western metaphysics or metalinguistics through a detour into the early Greek poetics encouraged his visitor to look back at the ancient root or etymology of the word for language in his native tradition, and to bring out and articulate the cosmological dimension of language in poetic images. Conversely, Tezuka's articulation of language as a cosmic event in terms of the aesthetics of *iki* and poetic imagery helped Heidegger to realize that his early work on Greek arts and poetics that runs parallel to Far Eastern thinking. Thinking along with his visitor, Heidegger began to see language in a cosmic light that seems to carry a much wider range of possibilities than its perceived ontological property—the house of Being—allows. As a result, toward the end of the dialogue, Heidegger decided to drop his first language metaphor and replace it with "Saying." Language as Saying, according to Heidegger, means that language shows and let the world appear. To show and let something appear is to let it "shine, but in the manner of hinting."[31]

Before we can jump to a conclusion that Heidegger and Tezuka have indeed reached a mutual agreement on the essential nature or being of language, we need to pause and take a look at an issue that the Dialogue overlooked. For instance, we need to consider how *koto*, as the constitutive part of the word for language, possesses such poetic and ontological status in the way that the Japanese think of language. And further, we need to consider how *koto* relates to *ba* or "leaves," as the two seemingly unrelated terms together designate the word for language.

We may recall that earlier in their conversation, Tezuka had briefly mentioned that the root meaning of *koto* is derived from two other words: *iro* and *ku*. He explained, while "*iro* means more than color and whatever can be perceived by the senses," *ku* stands for "the open, the sky's emptiness, means more than the supra-sensible."[32] The word *koto* derives its root meaning from the "interplay" of *iro* and *ku*. However, Tezuka did not provide any explanation for how *iro* or color—the word designates not only the physical color but anything perceived by the senses—relates to *ku*, the sky's emptiness, a word refers to something more than the suprasensible? Furthermore, how does the interplay of *iro* and *ku* give rise to the movement of language? As a non-Japanese speaker, Heidegger could not have any sense of what is missing here—the etymology of *koto ba*. The missing linkages certainly call for investigation here.

Etymologically, the two Japanese words *iro* and *ku* are the transliteration of two Chinese characters, *se* and *kong*, or "color" and "emptiness." *Se* and *kong* are in turn the transliteration of the two Sanskrit words, *rupa* and *sunyata*, "physical form" and "formlessness" or "emptiness," respectively, which are specific Buddhist terms of

Indian origin. In an attempt to capture the essential meaning of the Sanskrit words in an ideographical writing system, the Chinese transliterated the word *rupa* into *se* or "color," referring to physical color and any sense objects, and *sunyata* into *kong* or emptiness—sky-like emptiness, referring to a formless world without any sense objects. In the Chinese religious worldview, the notion of emptiness may be best captured in the image of the sky or Heaven, without spatial and temporal boundaries, and hence infinitely empty. The word *se*, not only refers to the color of the natural world but to desire over a perceived sensual object, especially sexually desire or lust. The word thus best captures the meaning of the word *rupa*, which is the first aggregate of a physical and psychological personality that was given birth to by human ignorance and desire. To summarize, we can say the etymology or root meaning of the Japanese words *iro* and *ku* are derived from the two Chinese words, *se* and *kong*, which in turn, are derived from the two Sanskrit words, *rupa* and *sunyata*. In the process of making their own writing system, as well as religious vocabularies, the Japanese coined these two Chinese ideographical characters with their original religious and cosmological dimensions.

Taking a detour we may now see how the Japanese term *koto ba* embodies a Buddhist worldview that sees the world as the interplay of color and emptiness—the to- and-fro movement from the sensible and physical world to a nonsensible and formless emptiness. In a Buddhist view, a being is repeatedly born and reborn into the world of senses and sense objects (the world of color and sense objects and sensual desires, or *samsara*) till it achieves liberation from that world. The false clinging to the physical world as if it had a permanent substance or self-nature perpetuates human attachment and suffering. To overcome the suffering, or rather the illusion and attachment to the sense world through vigorous mental, physical, and spiritual disciplines may lead to the eventual realization of the nonsubstantial, empty nature of the world.

We may now understand what Tezuka was trying to say about how the interplay of *iro* and *ku*, or the colorful and physical with the colorless and nonphysical, *mirrors* the movement of language. That is, akin to the constant interplay of *iro* and *ku*, in which sense-bound beings are constantly experiencing the alternating illusion and illumination of the true nature of the world as ultimately empty, language names the world in alternating movements of revelation and concealment of the true nature of what it names. That is, *koto*, in the manner of speaking and naming, discloses the to-and-fro movement and interaction between the illusionary world of colors, senses, and sense objects, and the formless and senseless and hence the empty nature of world.

There is no telling what would come out of the Dialogue if the visitor had pursued a discussion of both the etymological and spiritual root meaning of *koto* with Heidegger, as we have just outlined. However, we know with a degree of certainty that Heidegger would perhaps see a parallel between that of *iro ku* or *koto* as the alternating movement of the physical and the empty, with that of Being in the simultaneous motion of concealment and revelation. Tezuka indeed reminded him that his articulation of Being bears very close resemblance to the Eastern notion of emptiness; and that the movement of Being as the alternating revelation and concealment is also akin to that of language. Heidegger would perhaps not object to such an association. For he had stated that Being, among other things, is but a being-in-the-world that manifests itself in simultaneous movements of concealment and revelation. Language, akin to the notion of Being, indeed operates in a very similar manner. It "withholds its nature" and it "holds back when we speak it in the accustomed ways."[33] One may speculate that Heidegger may eventually get a good sense of these connections of the Eastern worldview embodied in the word for language his own thinking of Being and language. For, in the end, Heidegger reaffirmed that, echoing with the spirit of *koto*, that language as "Saying" is showing and revealing. Yet, it does that in a "manner of hinting," Heidegger specified, just like "your Japanese word *koto ba*," which "hints and beckons...."[34]

From the "house of Being" to "Saying," Heidegger was about to change his language metaphor. We may suggest a route to help with such a transition. At first glance, the image of a house does suggest a confined space enclosed by walls, windows, and doors. Yet, what encloses and confines also grants entry and exit. With accesses to the world outside, the residents of the one house could certainly reach the residents from the other houses. As comparative philosopher Graham Parkes put it, if the house is built in on the ground, as the cherry bosoms and leaves that are rooted in the earth, there would be infinite points of contact between the two language worlds.[35]

A Chinese Daoist view on the dynamic relation between confinement and openness, fullness and emptiness may also be helpful. From such a view, a house has to be empty; thereby it can be fully inhabited. The emptier the house is, the more it holds or contains. If the house is ultimately empty, it can house infinite numbers of beings; if all beings, non-beings, and entities are housed together in the emptiness of the house, there would be unlimited opportunities for contacts and connection. During the course of the conversation, Tezuka had spoken in such dynamic terms regarding the relation of confinement and openness to Heidegger. He suggested that the contact and connection between different groups of residents of the house of Being, or language worlds, are entirely possible, because "the site in which the kinship" between Japanese and German traditions is located at the "boundlessness which is shown to us in '*Ku*,'" or "the sky's emptiness."[36] In principle, Heidegger would not disagree with such a suggestion. For he had already reached an understanding that the Eastern notion of emptiness as an "essential being" is the other word for "nothingness" that needs to be added on to the Western thinking as "the other, to all that is present and absent."[37] To our knowledge, Heidegger may not have had an opportunity to reflect systematically how that can be done; he seemed to have understood what Tezuka attempted to explain to him in the dialogue. He stated, if the physical "site" for cross-cultural encounter takes place in the sky's vast emptiness that is without boundary, man would perhaps be able to walk "the boundary of the boundless."[38] Heidegger's paradoxical expression of walking the boundary of originally boundless indicates that he had not yet entirely given up the notion of boundary as confinement, restricting men residing in their respective linguistic and historical dwellings from contacting each other. Yet, he began to see the possibility that men could walk toward each other, by walking on the boundary of what was originally boundless.

Language as "the flower of the mouth"—Heidegger's New Language Metaphor

Heidegger continued to think about the nature of language along on the path pioneered in the dialogue with his Japanese visitor. His willingness to walk toward and even step over the boundary of the Far Eastern language world is reflected in his subsequent lectures on language; and in his new language metaphor. In a lecture called "The Nature of Language" delivered four years after the Dialogue, Heidegger stated:

> Language is the flower of the mouth. In language, the earth blossoms towards the blossoms of the sky.[39]

Heidegger had by now managed to establish a linkage in language that connects the earth and sky and their interactive movement with the human speech organ—the mouth. With Heidegger, language as speaking, the articulation of its sound through the mouth, becomes part of the cosmic movement, the blossoming and flowering of the earth and sky. As we can tell, language as "the flower of the mouth" comes much closer to the Japanese saying of language as "the petals that stem from *Koto*," or the petals that stem from the sky's emptiness.

It is obvious, Heidegger's preference for human speech, as part of the earthly movement that radically challenged the modern "metaphysical-technological" discount of spoken words as the "merely sensuous" side of language, in contrast unfavorably to writing, the embodiment of "the spirit of language." Heidegger argued that the reduction of human speech obscured a fundamental fact that the "spoken words of language" also "carry a meaning," just like "a property" of written language, for, they "ring and vibrate" and "hover and tremble" with the earth.[40] Heidegger's critique of the metaphysical reduction of human speech drew him closer than ever before to the Far Eastern thinking of the cosmic origin and the "earthy" nature of human language.

However, we still have to figure out how Heidegger managed to establish the connection between language, flower, mouth, the earth, and sky. And how did he attempt to articulate the interactive movement of the sky and earth, the flowering toward each other that eventually becomes the language movement itself—the flowing of the mouth. Similarly, we still have to bridge a gap left in Tezuka's account of the possible connection between *kota* and *ba*, which was also left out in the dialogue. That is, how does *ba*, the earthy movement—the flowing of the petals and leaves, interact with *koto*, the interaction of the sky's emptiness with the physical and colorful world of sense objects, which together gives rise to the movement of language? It seems that we need to figure out for both Heidegger and Tezuka in what manner does language or speech—the articulation of sounds through the human mouth—relate to the cosmic movement of the earth and heaven and eventually become part of the cosmic movement itself?

We shall first attempt to figure out how the linkage between *ba*, or leaves or petals, with *koto*, the sky's emptiness and its interactive movement with the colorful and physical world was created. Anyone who has some knowledge of the Japanese writing system may know that *koto ba*, read ideographically, is composed of two Chinese characters *yan* and *ye*, or words and leaves respectively. Borrowing the Chinese written scripts in creating their own writing, the Japanese chose the two Chinese written characters and combined them to designate what is called language.

One character is *yan* (word) and the other is *ye* (leaves). The way of compounding these two may be incomprehensible for those who are not familiar with the origin of Chinese writing system. According to mythology, writing was invented by the god *Fu Xi,* who developed ideograms by imitating the traces of birds flying across the sky and the footprints of animals on the ground. Thus the evolution of written characters was not the result of abstraction of the articulation of sounds by human speakers, but an "imitation" of the cosmic movement and the traces of animal movement, transmitted by the god. In the Chinese system, it is sufficient to use only the character *yan* or words to refer to language, including both spoken and written forms. Yet, in the Japanese writing system *ye* (leaves) is compounded with *yan* to designate the word for language. What would be the logic of combining these two unrelated characters to make the word for language? One way to figure out this puzzle is to examine the actual ideogram of the character *yan,* and as well as its verb form, *jiang* (to speak). Ideographically depicted, *yan* resembles a human mouth, from which the sound issues. The verb form *jiang* is a compound word that contains two characters: words and well.[41] Thus the word "to speak" denotes a parallel movement between the human articulation of sound from the mouth and water flowing out from the well. In other words, to speak is to let words flow out of the mouth in the same manner that water springs from the well. Apparently, the Japanese preserved this earthy link between words flowing out of the mouth and water springing from the ground by compounding the two seemingly unrelated words *koto* and *ba* together to designate language. The connection between the Chinese word *jiang* and the Japanese *koto ba* is as follows: language is that in which the words flow out from the mouth as water springs from the well under the ground, in Japanese, or as leaves or flower petals stem from the earth.

Incidentally, without any knowledge of Chinese or Japanese etymology discussed here, Heidegger was also able to establish a similar correlation between language, the human mouth, and earthly movement. Through a return to his native German dialects, Heidegger highlighted the "earthy" nature of language or human speech and its interactive movement with that of the earth and sky, by calling upon a long-ignored German word that tells the original meaning of German dialects. The various regional dialects in Germany are called *Mundarten,* which means "the modes of mouth," according to Heidegger. The different manners of speaking in different sections of the country suggest that the variations of speech from different local regions of the country are not merely a reflection of differences in "the organs of speech," but also the different movement and change in landscape and locality. Thus, Heidegger suggested that the old German dialects evolved over time, resulting in the difference in "the landscape and that means the earth," in words that were spoken differently each time."[42] In Heidegger's view it is the variations of locations and regions, which are part of the earth's movement, that give rise to the diverse speech patterns or dialects in different regions. Likewise, for Heidegger, the human mouth is not just an isolated organ of the body; similar to leaves, flowers, water and the well, all are "part of the earth's flow and growth in which we mortals flourish, and from which we receive the soundness of our roots."[43] Akin to the Chinese and Japanese accounts of the root meaning of language that speaks of a connection of cosmic and earthly movement with movement of the human mouth, Heidegger also managed to establish the linkage of the organ, of the mouth, through which sound was articulated and the earthly movement—the changing shapes and patterns of the landscape.

We may now offer a brief summary of the major thesis regarding the origin of language discussed in the dialogue. Heidegger and his visitor seemed to have reached some agreement on the flowing. Both of them agreed that in either German or Japanese traditions, language possesses an ontological property that claimed human beings who speak its tongue, and thus differentiates itself from the "linguistic signs" as treated in modern metalinguistics. The ontological and cosmic property of language, as Heidegger later agreed with the Japanese visitor, does not confine human speakers in the house of Being. It is rather a cosmic event or happening that allows them to maintain...and enriches the "face-to-face encounter of the world's regions,"[44] as Heidegger described. In Tezuka's words, language names the world and, in the event of naming, gives aesthetic pleasure to what is named in each unique moment, when the earth, leaves, petals, words, and human articulation of sounds are flowing into each other and become one another. For us, the mutual understanding of the "common" origin of human language seems to allow us to anticipate the possibility of a cross-cultural understanding. For, if there were a common language origin in both German and Japanese traditions, there might be an existing "shared" language world, regardless of the differences in actual speech of them respectively. Heidegger would perhaps not disagree with our speculation that there might be a shared and mutually intelligible language world. It seems that he had long ago hinted at such a possibility in *Being and Time.* He stated, "When we are explicitly hearing the telling of one another, we immediately understand what is said . . . in that we are already with him, in advance, among the entities which the telling is about. . . . What we primarily do not hear is the pronunciation of the sounds."[45] The message that Heidegger sent out seemed to be that, according to one of his commentators, if speaking to one another allows being-with others becomes explicitly "shared," the shared language community should be a manifestation of a "co-affectedness and a co-understanding," and what is "unshared" is "something that has not been taken hold of and appropriated."[46] However, since for both Heidegger and his visitor, language indeed appropriates in the ways in which it brings "man to its own usage."[47] In a manner of speaking, we may suggest, if any cross-cultural conversation were to be conducted in such a language, it would allow the speakers to bring themselves ever closer to the earthly nature and onto-cosmic origin of their existence in which the language they speak is a part.

Chapter 4

ON THE WAY TO A
CROSS-CULTURAL HERMENEUTICS

> Hermeneutics means neither the theory of the art of
> interpretation nor interpretation itself, but rather the
> attempt first of all to define the nature of interpreta-
> tion on hermeneutic grounds.
> —Martin Heidegger, "A Dialogue on Language"

We have demonstrated in the previous chapter that Heidegger and his
Japanese visitor seemed to have reached a mutual understanding that
there may be a "common" origin of language in both German and
Japanese traditions, and that what is being said in the conversation may
have already been understood prior to when the actual listening and
speaking take place. However, before we can clearly define the possibility
of this seemingly strange notion of cross-cultural understanding and dialogue, we need to take a look at Heidegger's appropriation of hermeneutics and hermeneutic relation here first. The discussion about the need to
reappropriate the concept and practice of hermeneutics and to disassoci-
ate the discipline from its modern framework constitutes an important
part of Heidegger's "Dialogue on Language." In this chapter we will seek
to determine if Heidegger's thinking would eventually allow a cross-cultural hermeneutic understanding to take place and a relationship between
German and Japanese traditions to emerge, if he were to suggest that
hermeneutics does not stand for "methodology of interpretation," and
that the hermeneutic relationship is a reciprocity of "supply and demand."

Heidegger Returns Hermeneutics to Its Greek Origin

During the Dialogue, the visitor, Tezuka, brought up the topic of
hermeneutics. He tells us that he had learned the concept through his

predecessor Count Kuki, who was then introducing Heidegger's theories of phenomenology and hermeneutics to Japanese students. Kuki perceived the possibility that these modern German conceptual frameworks might help to illuminate the Japanese artistic experience *iki*.[1] Instead of commenting on the cross-cultural interpretation of his theories and its instrumental value to a specific non-Western culture, Heidegger decided to explain to his current visitor the Greek origin of hermeneutics and the ways in which the term came to claim his imagination.

The root meaning of the word "hermeneutics" comes from an ancient Greek origin, according to Heidegger. Derived from the name Hermes, the messenger god who "brings the message of destiny," and the verb *hermeneuein* meaning "exposition," the word hermeneutics thus acquired the meaning of bearing a message and bringing "tidings." Later on, such "exposition becomes an interpretation of what has been said earlier by the poets who are the interpreters of the gods."[2] Therefore, in the Greek experience, hermeneutics was a more "playful thinking that is more compelling than the rigor of science,"[3] Heidegger pointed out. Having forgotten the etymological meaning of the word, the moderns reduced the Greek art of exposition as a way of bearing messages and tidings into a body of methodological knowledge of interpretation.

For Heidegger, the need to divorce hermeneutics from modern epistemology, for which methodology is a branch, is urgent. The knowledge of methodology is developed from study of the natural sciences. And to equate hermeneutics with science and epistemology, which allegedly granted the certainty of human knowledge about the world of texts, is pretentious in itself, according to Heidegger. For science makes its claim to knowledge by way of "method," and in the end, methodology takes precedence of science. When methodology was not perceived as a mere instrument serving the sciences, but as having "pressed the sciences into its own service,"[4] the perceived certainty of human knowledge became questionable. We may note here that Heidegger was echoing Nietzsche, who had already challenged the nineteenth century's preference for positivist and instrumental knowledge. Nietzsche had stated in his *Will to Power* that it is not victory of science, but the victory of scientific method over science that distinguished the century from the previous ones. Following Nietzsche, Heidegger continued to undermine the modern fixation on instrumental knowledge that had enclosed the practice of hermeneutics.

Heidegger suggested that the modern mistake could be rectified if the obscured ancient origin of hermeneutics could be revealed and restored to its original cultural context. One may then realize that hermeneutics is first of all an art rather than a science, and second, it is a bearing of message and tiding of one's own historical destiny—a form of self-understanding rather than an understanding of others, other texts, traditions, or peoples that could be observed from an objective distance. Returning hermeneutics to its original Greek cultural and religious context, Heidegger thus transformed the modern discipline from an epistemological interpretation of the other—other than oneself—to a radical ontological self-understanding of one's own destiny revealed in a message from the gods mediated by Hermes.

Heidegger did acknowledge that it was his predecessors who had initiated such an ontological shift. He mentioned to his visitor that the phenomenologists before him had objected against the modern conviction of the methodological status of hermeneutics, arguing that hermeneutics "does not have its usual meaning, methodology of interpretation, but means the interpretation itself."[5] For Heidegger, this means that hermeneutics is "neither the theory of the art of interpretation nor interpretation itself, but rather the attempt first of all to define the nature of interpretation on hermeneutic grounds."[6] What was then the hermeneutic ground from which interpretation originates? The question, Heidegger imagined, must relate to the question of Being. Heidegger related to his visitor that the path pioneered by the phenomenologists, inspired him to explore the question of Being. Like the origin of hermeneutics, the original meaning of Being was also lost through modern translation and interpretation. As the focus of Greek philosophical inquiries, the question of Being was essential to the search for hermeneutic ground. Yet, the original meaning of Being had been obscured because it was detached from its original context and the lifeworld. This lifeworld of Being, according to Heidegger, is the twofold, preontological state of being where "the Being of beings . . . the presence of present things" in virtue of "their simple oneness"[7] comes together. Whereas the modern epistemology or methodology maintains the absolute distinction between Being and beings, presence and present things, the hermeneutic approach, orientated toward self-understanding or the bearing of the message of one's own density in its original context, seems to allow the convergence of Being and beings and presence and present things to emerge.

It is tempting to assume that in Heidegger's thinking the return to the hermeneutic ground that man is expected to define is an ontological turn toward what had claimed his being—the message of his destiny. In other words, the hermeneutic ground could be the twofold world that claimed man as his destiny, that he is expected to retrieve and reveal. For, later, in the Dialogue, he explained, how the twofold world and man's relation to it mutually implicated, in such a manner, that the twofold world "makes its claim on man, calling him to its essential being."[8]

Heidegger Problematizes Man's Relation to the Twofold World

Heidegger explicitly reminded his visitor that, in his layout of the hermeneutic project, man no longer enjoyed a privileged position as an interpretive subject residing above the world of which he tries to gain an understanding. He is only a bearer of the message, as the twofold speaks to him,[9] bearing a relation to it "with respect to bringing tidings, with respect to preserving a message."[10]

Removing man from the center of the hermeneutical ground that he bears witness to and the message he is to retrieve, Heidegger next pointed out that man's hermeneutic relation to the twofold world does not reflect the everyday understanding of the term "relation." The word relation carries "a mathematical notation" that it is "empty and formal" on the one hand and calculative on the other, Heidegger points out. For him, such a conventional understanding of the term "relation" missed out on an important issue. That is, it leaves out "in what way, by what means, and from where the relation comes about, and what it properly is *qua* relation."[11]

Heidegger specified that man's hermeneutic relation to the twofold world was not an empty and formal concept; nor was it an instance of mutual dependence of the two entities in that one requires the other to fulfill its need. It is neither the instance quantified by a market-type of supply-and-demand, that is, man as a commodity who supplies himself to the demand of the twofold world, or vice versa.

However, in the Dialogue, Heidegger did not drop any hint on how to pursue a discussion of the relation between man and the twofold world in any positive terms. Instead, he only highlighted the self-revealing nature of the twofold world and its capability to reveal and unfold its own path in great clarity. The self-revealing nature of the twofold world seems to further negate any relevance of man to it. For he only responds and "thinks after" what was bestowed to him in the past that surely unfolds in his presence and possibly projects into his future. He listens to its appeal and yields to its call but cannot in any manner control its course and unfolding process.

The self-revealing nature of the twofold world may suggest a more radical possibility. That is, without man, there would still be the two-fold world and its message, unfolding itself. There would be neither meaning nor lack of it, since there is no empty space left to be filled up in the twofold world. Only with man, the one who lived in a receptive mode of attunement, could the message of the twofold reveal itself, only in "some finite and limited capacity."[12] Thus, the kind of relation that Heidegger allows man to have with the twofold would be a passive one, with man waiting and expecting, docilely and attentively, the unfolding of the message of his destiny. Indeed, a commentator on Heidegger pointed out that Heidegger's position on the subject indeed entails a strain of Oriental-style "quietism" and "passivity." Throughout his later writing, Heidegger constantly modified his position in order to avoid putting man in the stance of a "subject." He first speaks of man's receptive projection of the dimensions of lived time, whereby he both receives and projects the possibilities offered to him that make the texture of the world; and later, feeling such a description is still too "subjective," he simply states that man's "receptive standing" only means "to be human and aware."[13]

Does the self-revealing nature of the historical destiny that is bestowed upon man entirely exclude him from any active participation in its unfolding process? Could man have a hermeneutic relation with the twofold world at all? Apparently, Heidegger did not provide a direct answer to these questions, but only suggested to his visitor that, perhaps, they should not discard the conventional understanding of relation as a mutual need and a reciprocal exchange all together. Looking from a different angle, to be a "message-bearer of the message" of the twofold, is to be in a relation with it, as the latter "has always already offered itself to man."[14]

Thinking with Heidegger, we may infer that man must have had a prehistorical and preconceptual relation to the twofold world; and anyone who is attuned to the message of the twofold world, witnessing the unfolding process, must be *hermeneutical*. Heidegger would perhaps not disagree with us here, since, in his understanding, man as human *Dasien* had always and already understood itself and its world as an involved being-in-the-world and a being-with-the-other. However, the real question becomes, why did man overlook such a primordial fact that he was already listening to the message and that he had always borne a relation with the twofold world?

Heidegger's answer is that man usually "pays no particular attention to the fact that he is ever listening already to that message."[15] The lack of attention or awareness, Heidegger suggested inexplicitly, is due to the fact that man has not fully understood the direction and route he traveled to and from the message of the twofold world. Man is not tuned to the concept that, as a message bearer, he may have traveled from "the message," and at the same time, he "must have gone towards it."[16] To travel from whence he has gone could only be a journey of the circular route. For it is only through a circular movement that man could see his historical destiny, granted to him in the past, projected into the future, from the time of the present. It is indeed Heidegger's articulation of hermeneutics as a self-understanding of one's own historical destiny that has introduced a notion of the temporal-spatial circularity and simultaneity, which clearly differs from the conventional conception of time and space as having a linear and sequential movement. Within the linear and sequential time framework, an encounter with something in the past, present, and future tense *simultaneously* appears to be incomprehensible. And yet, given the circularity and simultaneity that Heidegger's hermeneutical movement permits, the seemingly impossible meeting with one's own destiny—a past, present, and future event at the same time actually becomes possible.

A look at Heidegger's notion of time in his later thought may help us to understand his hermeneutical worldview here. Stating it in another context, Heidegger suggested that what we define as time is a spatial movement that is "simultaneously the has-been, presence, and the present that is waiting for our encounter and is normally called future."[17] It is only through this notion of time that man could capture "the mutual interdependence or correlativity" between "multiple dimensions of all historical existences and the object of thought."[18] Heidegger here projected a revolutionary vision of time that encompassed the multiple dimensions of historical existences and the object of thought and man in their mutual dependence and correlation. Embracing such a vision of time, Heidegger suggests, we would overcome the oversight of linear time, which only moves in "the successions of 'nows' one after the other as elements of parametric time, one 'now' is never in open face-to-face encounter with another."[19] The absence of the encounter in turn explains why man remains unaware of the route of his journey to and from the historical destiny that had claimed his Being and that he is expected to retrieve.

Unfortunately, Heidegger did not discuss his vision of time in the Dialogue, which could have otherwise helped to illustrate the circular movement of the hermeneutic understanding of the twofold world and the route of the journey that man takes to and from his own historical destiny. Realizing the challenge that his notions of time and hermeneutic movement may pose, Heidegger only cautiously suggested that the relation between man and the twofold world still remained veiled and that man had not yet learned "the gift" to retrieve the message of "the unconcealment of the twofold."[20]

"Fallenness among beings," a Negative Mode of Cross-Cultural Encounter

Given man's relation with his historical destiny still remains veiled and that he has not learned the gift to retrieve its message, could Heidegger eventually allow a relation between men as fellow messengers who may happen to be listening to a similar message? Specifically, could there have been already an actual hermeneutic relation between the German and Japanese traditions before the instance of the Dialogue where Heidegger and Tezuka were brought together as fellow messengers? We are not alone in our speculations. Heidegger's commentators have also attempted to figure out what exactly, or what specific modes, would Heidegger allow in an East-West hermeneutic relationship?

For instance, David Kolb, in his comments on Heidegger's place in the history of modernity, suggested that Heidegger would have to grant an East-West relation if he acknowledges the possibility of the happening of the "appropriate event" or *Ereignis*. According to Kolb, Heidegger once used *das Ereignis* as "a prelude" to the modern technology that brings man and things together. It is in *"Ereignis"* that "the possibility opens for us" for overcoming "the simple dominance of universal imposition in a more original happening."[21] According to Kolb, the anticipation of this more primary happening or event must have already implied a possibility of a cross-cultural relationship. For the event of appropriation requires "the deeply divergent traditions" to coexist, with each being "dominated by a different meaning of being." The idea that traditions may coexist, in turn, "highlights the discontinuity implicit in the primacy of the appropriate event."[22] Further, Kolb continued to speculate, in spite of the fact that "the unconcealment of the being of things" in each tradition is radically different from that of the other, there would always be a possibility of the convergence of differently granted historical traditions, because in each, there is "an inner multiplicity" in what is opened up to that of the other.[23] Such an "inner multiplicity" within different traditions provides points of contact, allowing certain aspects of one tradition to interact with and assimilate that of the other. For instance, in the case of the Japanese tradition, there existed perhaps an "inner multiplicity" and "a rhythm of openness and closure" that makes it easier for the Japanese to "take in Western ways," and thereby allows them to live more fruitfully in a world in which "the traditional and Western ways of life conflict and interpenetrate."[24] In contrast to the Japanese tradition, there seems to be a lack of such a multiplicity and rhythm of openness in the Chinese tradition that has made modern China's encounter with the West more difficult.

There are some other comparative philosophers who supported Kolb's observation. Graham Parkes, in the introduction to his edited book *Heidegger and Asian Thought*, observed that there is indeed a "pre-existent harmony" between Heidegger's thinking and the Far Eastern classical traditions. Yasuo Yuasa, a contributor to Parkes's edited volume, testified that at the turn of the twentieth century, Japanese intellectuals indeed held Germany as "the Mecca of philosophy." There were several Japanese students and scholars who journeyed to the southwestern universities in Germany to study German philosophies, and the University of Heidelberg, where Heidegger was teaching, became the center of the attraction.[25]

However, did Heidegger also perceive a similar rhythm of openness and closure in the Western traditions, or in his own system of thought, which anticipates a fruitful interaction with the Eastern or Japanese traditions? Is the intellectual attraction mutual and reciprocal? According to Kolb, Heidegger did not seem to think so. Heidegger once remarked that the West could corrupt the East but the East cannot save the West. Kolb suspected that Heidegger must have thought that "the West's granting of presence could threaten the East without there being any influence for good in the other direction."[26] The West, with its metaphysics and technology, could lead the East to a fall; but the East, with its Zen Buddhism and Daoism, could not cure the disease of the West or prevent it from the fall. Hence for Heidegger, even if there were a relation between the East and West, it could only be an asymmetrical one, Kolb commented. This East-West asymmetry can be easily explained. According to Kolb, the later Heidegger no longer regarded metaphysics and technology as the manifestation of an exclusively Western destiny, but as the general "human situation as such."[27] Hence, the mode of "fallenness among beings" that the West has suffered from would have also inflicted the Eastern or Asian traditions. If "fallenness remains a more basic or fundamental characterization than metaphysics," and "every world is liable to the fallenness amid beings," Kolb concluded, the human fallenness "levels out what has been granted and forgets the appropriative event and its withdrawal."[28]

Interestingly, Kolb here also mentioned the peculiar East-West asymmetry that was observed by other comparative philosophers, as we discussed in the previous chapters. However, Kolb did not offer further explanation as to why the fall is a more "basic" mode of human existence; and the "similar fallen debased modes" that level out the difference between the two traditions cannot also be the way to level out what was granted to them—such as the potential to heal and grow.[29] Nor did he discuss what had led Heidegger to decide that the Western and Eastern worlds share a similar mode of the fall, presumably, one metaphysical and technological, and the other, the nonmetaphysical and nontechnological. What Kolb had inferred from Heidegger's position is that, since the Eastern and Western traditions differ in their respective "deep authentic possibilities," therefore, for the purposes of "healing and growing," each had to look into its own tradition for cures.[30]

Given the thematic ambiguities left in commentary given both by Heidegger and his commentators on the East-West relation, we are left wondering if there would be other ways to conceptualize the mode of East-West encounter. For instance, if we were to agree with Heidegger that metaphysics and technology are no longer limited to the histories and the destiny of the West but have become a universal imposition on the Eastern part of the world, and that in them lie the very possibility of a more original happening, the East should also be standing in anticipation, like the West, for a more primordial instance that promises to overcome the fall from metaphysics and technology. If so, why couldn't there be a common interest and a joint effort to retrieve that instance?

Do Metaphysics and Technology Necessarily Lead the East to the Fall?

To think otherwise than both Heidegger and his commentators is to transgress the limits that their thinking imposes onto themselves. For instance, we may outline a condition of the possibility for a more positive mode of East-West connection than that of fallenness among beings. In fact, Heidegger and Tezuka's dialogue on language had set a positive example for a constructive cross-cultural encounter. As we may recall, through painstaking effort, they had eventually succeeded in retrieving a "common" language origin that indeed pointed toward a possibility of overcoming the tradition of the metalinguistics, which seemed to be what had divided the different language worlds. The traditional Japanese thinking and perception of the language world and artistic experience proved to be able help Heidegger to "step back" from the fall—the fall from metalinguistics. In fact, this primordial origin of language did not become intelligible to either Heidegger or Tezuka till the moment of their dialogical encounter and till the time when we were able to provide some missing information to fill the thematic gaps in the development of languages in the East Asian world. Based upon such positive experience, we have no reason not to be hopeful that we may be able to reconstruct Heidegger and Tezuka's conversation on metaphysics and technology by reconsidering and clarifying some of the dialogue's assumptions about the subject. As Kolb himself had observed, Heidegger's articulation of hermeneutics as the bearing and retrieving of the message of one's destiny sent out an important "message of hope." That is, metaphysics and technology, though as system of thought, had completed in themselves, are not the final destiny of humankind; a premetaphysical and primordial instance—the world of the twofold—is on its way.

To demonstrate that such a primordial instance is retrievable and a positive mode of cross-cultural relation attainable, we may first want to clarify the assumptions that Heidegger and his visitor made that Western metaphysics and technology were merely negative forces that necessarily lead the Japanese tradition to the fall.

We will take a close look at a Japanese reaction to Western metaphysics and technology, mediated by Tezuka's narrative in the Dialogue. Tezuka related to Heidegger that European metaphysics and the categories of aesthetics in fact presented "great temptation" to Japanese thinkers at the time that they were attempting to reexamine and reconstruct their traditional artistic experiences and poetics. Since the time of Kuki, Japanese thinkers had imagined that Western aesthetics and the conceptual framework may "give a higher clarity" to the understanding of *Iki*—an artistic style developed in the Edo period—and give an aid to comprehending "what is of concern to us as art and poetry."[31] Despite his own skepticism toward using Western metaphysical terms to interpret Japanese aesthetic experiences, Tezuka admitted that it was indeed difficult not to explain *Iki* in terms of Western aesthetic categories or to "define it metaphysically."[32]

What made Western metaphysics attractive and problematic at the same time for Japanese thinkers? What did they see in the conceptual framework and categories offered by modern European aesthetics that would help with the reconstruction and illumination of native traditions? To put it differently, what was perceived as obscured in the traditional Japanese world of art and poetry that would need clarification?

Interestingly, Tezuka himself actually offered an answer to the questions mentioned previously without, perhaps, self-awareness. In his discussion of traditional Japanese theater, Noh, with Heidegger, Tezuka stated that there appeared to be a lack of means in traditional theater to differentiate poetic objects situated in different dimensional space. In his words, there was an absence of "the delimiting power to represent objects related in an unequivocal order," that is, "above and below each other."[33] Such a perceived lack became more pronounced when it encountered European film technology and photography. Contrary to film, Noh has only an empty stage with one actor making gestures to indicate the unfolding of plot and the changing of scenery. For instance, to announce the appearance of a mountain, the actor needs only to "slowly raise his open hand and [hold] it quietly above his eyes at eyebrow level,"[34] and only to use a slight additional gesture to cause "mighty things to appear out of a strange stillness."[35]

However, this traditional performing art and theater did not appear to be easily replaced by modern Western photography and the film industry, Tezuka stated. He related to Heidegger that the Japanese did not import Western film technology without any skepticism. For example, he explained that though the film camera better illuminates and differentiates poetic objects at different dimensions of space, yet, the differentiating power of the camera also greatly obscures and even distorts the lifeworld of ancient Japan. Take the early Japanese movie *Rashomon*, for example. (It turns out that Heidegger happened to have read something about Noh and viewed the movie *Rashomon*). In the film, the camera "captured and imprisoned" the Japanese lifeworld for the "sole purpose of photography."[36] It sets the lifeworld of ancient Japan in a frame by focusing and bringing some scenes to the foreground, pushing back and marginalizing the others into the background. Whereas the foreground looks like the world of the European or American, it was only the background of the filmed world that remained traditionally Japanese.[37] Tezuka thus concluded that the production of the movie *Rashomon* was a convincing example that illustrates the unfolding process of what Heidegger had described as Europeanization and technicalization of the earth and man.

We will pause and reflect on Tezuka's narrative here for a moment. For him, it seems, the very capability of the film camera to focus, highlight, and hence to differentiate poetic objects at different dimensional spaces *simultaneously* fulfills the lack in traditional theater and distorts and even conceals the lifeworld of ancient Japan. Therefore, whereas the temptation to use film technology to illuminate and differentiate poetic objects was real, the feeling that the latter may distort and obscure the lifeworld was also present. This simultaneous attraction and aversion toward the modern technology of photography on the part of the Japanese may be very significant. For it is not simply a self-conflicting and hence illogical feeling, but an indicator of a range of mixed attitudes and perspectives that usually accompany the process of cross-cultural reference and borrowing. More importantly, it may reflect the peculiar nature of modern technology itself. (Heidegger elsewhere addressed this topic, which unfortunately, was not brought into the Dialogue.)

It appeares that in their conversation, both Heidegger and Tezuka are preoccupied with undermining the perceived negative impact of the universal imposition of the technological domination of the earth and man in general and "all-consuming Europeanization" of traditional Japanese society in particular.[38] The preoccupation prevented Heidegger from incorporating his reflection of the nature of modern technology with the discussion of the film industry in the Dialogue. Briefly stated here, Heidegger had discussed elsewhere how modern technology, as a way of setting up the world into a frame, simultaneously reveals and conceals the world it perceived and processed. Yet, it is in this double movement of revealing and concealing from which emerges the possibility of opening up a primordial world of the twofold in which the thinking or recollection of Being could be an embodied experience. Such a preoccupation also prevented him from attempting an understanding of the significance of using body and hand gestures on the empty stage in the Noh play and brings the Japanese artistic expression to a comparison with his own exploration of the ontological dimension of the hand and hand gesturing, discussed elsewhere. This same preoccupation also hindered Tezuka from exploring the ontological dimension of hand gestures and body positioning in the Noh play as an expression of the embodiment of experiences deeply rooted in Eastern spiritual and ascetic traditions. In the end, contrary to what Tezuka attempted to show to Heidegger—that *Rashomon* was an powerful example of the ever-increasing Europeanization of the earth—Heidegger only saw in the movie the foreign, mysterious, and charming world of ancient Japan, otherwise inaccessible to him without filming and photography. In fact, the inadequate discussion of the nature of technology and the hand gestures as an ontological and embodied experience leads them to make a hasty conclusion that "the Eastasian world, and the technical-aesthetic product of the film industry are incompatible."[39]

As we can see here, unlike previous discussion of the topic of language that had yielded to a mutual understanding and a fusion of horizon, the current conversation yields to the perceived binary opposites of the traditional theater and the modern film, the photographical representation and the gestures as embodiment of the world perceived, and of course, of the East and West.

To by-pass these perceived binary opposites, we need to bring into the Dialogue Heidegger's own reflection on the nature of technology, as well as the Eastern understanding of the ontological and cosmological dimensions of body posture and hand gesture as embodied experiences. Bringing in the two missing pieces, we may be then able to demonstrate that Western film technology and traditional Japanese theater are not *fundamentally* different from each other, as Heidegger and Tezuka had assumed, if modern film technology could be reversed and brought back to a pretechnological world—a primordial world where Being was not a metaphysical construct but an embodied existence; and the recollection of Being could be a hand gesture or a bodily movement.

First, let us take a look at Heidegger's reflection on the nature of modern technology. According to Heidegger, technology at the present age was no longer the application of scientific research to a manufacturing process, in which man uses a tool to devise a product. It rather became an automatic setting up, or enframing, of the world, in which man, things, and objects were brought together and exposed to a maximum level of clarity. The technological framing of the world would eventually reduce the lifeworld to a stock, a fund, or a supply, fully exposed for any exhaustive extraction. And yet Heidegger also reminded us that modern technology as such also reached the ultimate limit of concealing Being and obscuring of things. That is, in its way of concealing the world through a certain set up, technological framing also reveals the world it perceived and set up. Heidegger summarized this seemingly paradoxical nature of modern technology in the following terms: "the essence of modern technology lies in enframing. Enframing belongs within the destiny of revealing."[40] If, technological enframing as a concealment of Being had reached its ultimate limit, the disclosure and revealing of Being and things must have also reached the maximum level of clarity. In the end, Heidegger seemed to suggest that the concealment and revelation are no longer distinguishable.[41] Gaining a good understanding of the nature of modern technology and the way it operates, one begins to see the possibility for overcoming technological modernity.

Interestingly enough, it is one of his Japanese commentators who spelled out the ways in which Heidegger had managed to illustrate this curious relation of the revealing and concealing of modern technology. In his commentary on Heidegger's Bremen lectures on technology comprised of four pieces: "The Thing," "The Enframing," "The Danger," and "The Turning," Keiji Mizoguchi spelled out an inner logic and a cyclical motion around which Heidegger's four lectures were arranged. He suggested that in the lecture series, Heidegger did not treat technology or enframing as a mere danger that subsequently leads to the fall; but that which entails a turn, a turn away from danger, and hence a step back to a primordial world to the world of things. That is to say, the turning away from technology as a danger—the danger of enframing the world, enables a turn to a thing. A thing, in Heidegger's vocabulary, differs from an object, while the latter was subjected to scientific investigation and technological treatment, the former manages to exist in its tangible and concrete form. Hence, a thing stands for a pretechnological and primordial world where Being and beings and the presence and present things are in their simple oneness.

To apprehend Heidegger's thinking on technology in these four lectures, Mizoguchi suggested that we must familiarize ourselves with an alternative conceptual framework—that is the cyclical view of the world movement and encounter. Because it is only with such a nonlineal motion, the "primordial (*anfanglich*) earliness shows itself to man only at the end," and "the world ... presented in 'The Thing' is at once the last element and the earliest origin."[42]

Heidegger has developed a vision of a pretechnical and primordial world that the thing presents, based on the mythological and pre-Socratic Greek worldview, as Heidegger's Japanese commentator observed. For Heidegger, in such a world, "the earth and heaven, mortals and gods are constantly and reciprocally reverting, particularized into their individual beings, and at the same time unified in their nature—a world of mirror-play."[43] In such a fourfold world, the sky and earth, gods and mortals were not *crossing over* but *crossing through* each other; and Being was the locus where the fourfold world of beings were intersecting and crossing through one another (here, the twofold world is expanded into the fourfold world). In Heidegger's vision, this primordial world that modern technology—as simultaneous concealing and revealing movement would eventually lead to—was to be a corporeal and mutually embedded existence, where the perception and recollection of Being and the world of beings became one and the same embodied experience.[44]

At this point, we may suggest that if the film camera can effectively illuminate and reveal, as well as obscure and conceal, the lifeworld of ancient Japan *simultaneously*, the issue for the Japanese is not to reject film photography or to go back to the empty stage of the Noh play, but rather to work out a way to rethink the operation of the camera in terms of its pretechnical origin and context, where there were no objects out there to be objectified and photographed, but only things existing as such in their concrete and tangible forms, to be handled by hands, and hence, hand gestures.

Hand Gesture, Embodiment, and a Positive Mode of Cross-Cultural Understanding

Although Heidegger projected a primordial instance as the fourfold world and offered a description of its characteristics and dynamics, he remained inexplicit about the route of return—the return from the modern technological to a pretechnological or primordial world of the fourfold. The question of how the leap from the technological segregated world to a mutually embedded existence takes place remained a problem rather than a solution in Heidegger's thinking. As some comparative philosophers observed, Western intellectual and spiritual traditions had largely ignored and excluded the body and embodiment experience from the paradigm of knowledge and religious experiences; and Heidegger, just breaking free from the grip of these traditions, still "leaves the embodiment of thinking largely un-thought."[45] Given the situation, it thus becomes necessary to call upon Eastern thinking of the body, bodily movement, and embodiment experiences. Both David M. Levin and Hwa Yol Jung, contributors to the collection: *Heidegger and Asian Thought*, suggested in their respective articles that if Eastern thinking of experiences of the body and embodiment, cultivated in their ancient spiritual traditions, could be brought into the dialogue with Heidegger's thought, the stepping back from the metaphysical and technological dominated world, and return to a more authentic existence become more visible.[46] In Eastern traditions, the cosmos or universe is an organic, living, and dynamic whole—an integrated and mutually embedded existence; and a human body is the embodiment of the various realms this cosmos—physical, spiritual, and natural worlds. For instance, as Levin pointed out, a hand gesture in the Tibetan Buddhist *mudra* is not an external expression of response to a divine Other, but is itself an access to the "a primordial awareness of the intrinsic openness of Being" and an activation of that "ontological awareness that has already existed" in the "corporal world and the embodied existence."[47]

To explore this line of thinking, we may adopt a different view on the hand gesture and the body positioning in the traditional Japanese Noh. We may suggest that the hand gesture of the actor is not a representation of the appearing of a mountain, but is itself a temporal and special state of being of the mutually embedded lifeworld where man and mountain are virtually one. The ontological nature of the hand gesturing leaves no conceptual and existential gap between the appearing of the mountain and the actor's hand and body; and the raising of a hand to the level of the eyebrow embodies, and in the end becomes, the movement of the mountain itself. This may sound foreign to an artist schooled in the modern European traditions. Yet, to achieve convergence of man and nature, or the mutual transformation of the two in the artist's creative expression in the classical Far Eastern tradition is very possible. To realize such an aspiration, classical Chinese aesthetic theory instructs that one needs to go through a contemplative process of *wuhua*, or "to become one with the objects that one portrays." The undergoing of such a process found its inspiration in Daoist thought. Zhuang Ze's account of himself being transformed into a butterfly and the butterfly into himself is perhaps the most familiar story to Western readers. In fact, Far Eastern poetics regarded that only when the division or boundary between the artist and the objects he or she portrays gets dissolved does the creative imagination and artistic expression reach a degree of perfection. The process of *wuhau* may suggest two modes of transcendence. In the first, "man gives himself over to the world and its ultimate futile aims"; and in the second, seeing "the fleeting character of the world," he gives himself over to "his . . . existential possibilities in the face of transcendence." In both modalities, "man strays away from 'existence' into mere 'organismic being.'"[48] D. T. Suzuki, in his *Essays in Zen Buddhism*, also speaks of the desirability of man's becoming one with nature; and that it is that oneness that enables man to give spiritual and enlightened response to the world around him, which, in his view, is embodied in "the rise of the eyebrows, winks of the eyelids, and moves of the hand and legs."[49]

Gaining some understanding of Far Eastern poetics and cosmological worldview, one may better understand Tezuka's remarks on the hand gesture used in the Noh play as that which enables a "... gathering," which "unites itself with what we bear to it and what it bears to us"; and it is "in and through" this mutual encounter and gathering that "the mountains appear."[50] Heidegger did not respond to Tezuka's comment on the use of the hand gesture, but only commented that, the hand gesture may indeed help us experience what is here and now. Here, what appeals to Heidegger is the immediacy or physical proximity that a gesture carries to what it bears here and now.

In fact, elsewhere, Heidegger had discussed the hand movement in relation to thinking, and the recollection of Being as an embodied experience. In his essay on "What Is Called Thinking," Heidegger spoke of how the hand movement bears the element of thinking. He stated, "Every motion of the hand in every one of its works carries itself through the element of thinking; every bearing of the hand bears itself in that element. All the world of the hand is rooted in thinking."[51] Here, as we can clearly see, Heidegger's thinking actually runs a close parallel with Tezuka's account of the hand gesture. In both cases, a hand is no longer separated from the thinking being, nor from the world it gathers and bears. In fact, the hand gesture bears itself to the thinking being and the world that it moves and reaches and eventually becomes the embodiment of thinking, which is what Heidegger calls the recollection of Being as being-in-the-world and being-with-others.

Technology, Karma, and Fate: A Common Ground of East-West Encounter

To further explore the possibility of returning to the primordial world, some Japanese thinkers suggested that we may want to think of what ultimately gives rise to modern technology in the first place. Although Heidegger had satisfactorily described how technology worked by ways of setting up the world, he did not address specifically what leads to this kind of constant making, doing, and acting upon the world. As Akihiro Takeichi, another contributor to *Heidegger and Asian Thought*, observed, "Heidegger does not question why and how 'projection of the world,' 'making,' and 'revealing' emerge." Instead, what he offered is a phenomenological account of technology as an already-existing event, in that "man . . . constantly acts and carries out the projection of the world."[52]

For some Japanese thinkers, this "oversight" on what causes technology to happen could be corrected if the perspective of a Buddhist understanding of karma was brought into the discussion. According to Takeichi, the Buddhist teaching of karma and the explanation of how karmic effects were accumulated could perhaps fill in the blank space left in Heidegger's treatment of the subject. For, karma literally means acting, making, or doing. However, it is not the first cause or an end in itself. Karma is only the second limb of the "Twelve Link Causality," alternatively called the doctrine of "Dependent Origination," intended to explain how the conditioned world of birth, death, and rebirth, or *samsara*, comes into being. That is, karma or action is further explained by the link that precedes it, which is called ignorance. Ignorance is the concealment of the knowledge of how the world of *samsara* comes into being and the way it perpetuates and sustains itself, which gives rise to blind actions and reactions carried out in the world. In other words, humankind's habitual action and making is the eventual acting out of that ignorance; and it is ignorance that gives rise to the conscious or unconscious doings and makings. Takeichi further suggested that technology as a chain of actions and reactions is self-sustaining, because it is fed on the never-ending desire and perceived need to chase more and better technological innovations—the ignorance of its ultimate cause. As long as the ignorance remains unremoved, the blind actions— karmic or technological—will continue to frame up human beings and their world, only to ensure further actions and desires for more actions.

It is only viewed in the light of the Buddhist teaching of karma, that technology could become a universal imposition. For the Japanese, the novelty or absurdity of technology is not due to the absence of an encounter with the new, or modern, but is only a reminder of how things could be encountered in a habitual way—a constant making and doing without knowing how and why—the working of the accumulated karmic effects. To conclude, Takeichi suggested that the ignorance that precedes karma and that gives rise to a series of actions and reactions with their accumulated results eventually and inevitably lead to a form of nihilism—devaluing of what is the most valuable. Takeichi's solution to this seemingly hopeless human condition is a religious one. It is only through religious transcendence that we may one day arrive at a self-awareness that "Being is immediately 'danger' and life is immediately sinful," and hence the need to pray for Buddha Amida's grace and deliverance. It is only then that human beings, in the East or West, can be saved.[53]

In his essay on "The Question Concerning Technology," Heidegger seemed to speak in similar terms. "Technology is the fate of our age," where fate means "the inevitableness of an unalterable course."[54] In such a view, technology or technical modernity has already claimed man and become part of his being so decisively, that as a man he has no choice but to be claimed so at any time.[55] For Heidegger, this explains why the "Europeanization of the earth and man" is happening now. Man voluntarily takes part in this technological ordering of the world that had claimed his being and conditioned his existence. He answers the call of this universal imposition and acts within a range of possibilities that were presented to him. Residing within this network of temporality that solicits and challenges him to further activity,[56] man constantly projects himself upon the world, which in turn further conditions his being and mode of existence. As such, the way technology works stands in a close proximity to the working of karma. It is no wonder why Heidegger eventually appeals to the hope that the overcoming of technological imposition indeed requires a religious solution—the help of a god.

PART IV.
A CONCEPTUAL
DIALOGUE WITH
HEIDEGGER'S TEXT
ON HERMENEUTICS

Chapter 5

HEIDEGGER'S ONTOLOGICAL HERMENEUTICS AS A WORLDVIEW AND WORLD ENCOUNTER

> In our indicative definition of the theme of hermen-
> eutics, facticity = in each case our own *Dasein* in its
> being-there for a while at the particular time.
> —Martin Heidegger, *Ontology—*
> *The Hermeneutics of Facticity*

In this chapter, we will further explore Heidegger's hermeneutic theory by initiating a conceptual dialogue with his text, *Ontology—The Hermeneutics of Facticity*. The text was developed from his lecture series on phenomenology and hermeneutics delivered in the summer of 1923, three years prior to the publication of his groundbreaking work, *Being and Time*. The English translation of the German text only became available in 1999. For whatever reasons, the text managed to escape the attention of the commentators of Heidegger, as well as that of comparative philosophers, some of whom have regarded Heidegger's hermeneutic theory as instrumental in developing a model for cross-cultural understanding and dialogue.

We shall suggest that the text is not only an introduction to Heidegger's first and most important work, *Being and Time*, but an indispensable piece on the twentieth century hermeneutic theory itself. It radically transformed the tradition of the discipline from a body of instrumental knowledge—methodology of interpretation—into a form of ontology of being-in-the-world and seeing the world—a worldview. Without relying on a metaphysical a priori to sustain an absolute distinction between the world as *it is* and the world as *it is perceived* and an epistemological dualism of subject and object, Heidegger managed to develop a new conceptual framework for investigating the world of phenomena and a nonmetaphysical and nondualistic language to describe what is being investigated as a movement or moving reality—temporal, transitory by nature, capable of assuming different modes of expression at a particular point of time.

Our objectives here are to piece together and reconstruct an onto-logical hermeneutic theory, outlined but not systematically presented by Heidegger himself in his lecture, and spell out a radically different worldview implicated by it by bringing it into focus with a Buddhist outlook of the world, which also perceives the latter as a moving reality—constantly changing and without an inherent self-nature. A parallel reading of these two historically and culturally specific onto-hermeneutic worldviews may shed some light onto the perplexity and ambiguity generated by the metaphysical and dualist thinking of subject and object, self and other, and East and West in the recent debates on comparative philosophy and East-West relation, examined in the previous chapters. Looking through a different pair of lenses, in the end, one may eventually see the instances of cross-cultural encounter as the world movement—a dynamic, co-originated, interdependent, and simultaneous happening, without a preconceived notion of a theometaphysical presence.

Heidegger Departs from Husserl's Phenomenology

Heidegger's lecture series: "Ontology—The Hermeneutics of Facticity," outlines some possibilities for developing a new hermeneutic project, through an revaluation of the modern phenomenological tradition, represented by Edmund Husserl's landmark work, *Logical Investigation*. For the sake of conceptual clarity, we shall look at the second part of the lecture first, in which, we may see how Heidegger assessed Husserl's work from which he both draws insight for his new thinking on hermeneutics and marks a point of departure.

As usual, Heidegger started out to reevaluate a modern discipline by looking into the ancient etymological roots of its certain key words or terms. To discuss the discipline of phenomenology, he began with the investigation of the Greek origin of the word *phenomenon*. The root meaning of the word *phenomenon*, in the ancient Greek vocabulary, means that something "shows itself from itself" in a "distinctive mode of being-an-object."[1] Derived from its root meaning, phenomenology—the modern disciplinary research, appropriated by Kant, came to mean the description of the conditions of possibility in which an "object just as it shows itself and only to the extent that it shows itself."[2] As such, it differentiates itself from the other research methods employing the methods of induction, deduction, inference, and so on. Since phenomenology only "describes, but does not construct," the modern phenomenologist such as Husserl called it a "descriptive psychology."[3]

Heidegger relates that in his *Logical Investigation*, Husserl limited his phenomenological investigation to the objects of logic, such as concepts, propositions, assertions, and so on. His primary concern was to identify "where are the objects about" from which "logic speaks and how are they there for it."[4] With Husserl, the object to be investigated was reduced into what is found in the conscious experiences only, or rather, in a pure consciousness, equated with intentionality. Consequently, Heidegger pointed out, the disciplinary practice was "narrowed down to mean consciousness as an object,"[5] and its language into that of mathematics—the language of the natural sciences, which, Husserl assumed, would guarantee the objectivity of his phenomenological investigation.

Heidegger was, on the one hand, impressed by Husserl's project, seeing the new possibilities of looking at objects as they "come to be defined just as they give themselves," which were not available in the conventional metaphysics and, on the other, dissatisfied with Husserl's reduction of the phenomenon into that of a consciousness object and elevating phenomenology to "the level of mathematic rigor." To be able to utilize the phenomenological strategies for investigation and yet at the same time avoid its reductive tendency, Heidegger decided that the etymological meaning of the word "phenomenon" needed to be reexamined and that the modern discipline of phenomenology needed to be detached from the grip of the natural sciences and the alleged status of universality.

Heidegger argued that, in light of early Greek thinking, a phenomenon—something that shows itself from itself as an object in a distinctive mode—could only be "a material thing in space."[6] With phenomenon being defined as such, the phenomenological investigation should not start with the conscious experience of an object, but with what Heidegger referred to as the material objects in the field. To illustrate his point, Heidegger provided a sample phenomenological analysis of his family table (to be replaced by a public hammer later). The table as an object that shows itself from itself is not a mental image

or concept available only for conscious processing and logical investigation, but a material thing, assuming specific characteristics and func-
tionalities, belonging to a specific family. Thus, to approach it is not to
reduce it into an object of consciousness and intentionality, but to treat
it as a temporal being-in-the-world, useful and beautiful and so on, *as* it
is looked at by specific family members at a particular time. Thus,
Heidegger concluded that the essential being of the table lies in its
"temporality of everydayness," that is, "something that one can do
something with."[7]

Here, we can see Heidegger stepping away from the direction that
Husserl's *Logic of Investigation* was pointing to. While Husserl
attempted to identify an object with that of the conscious and intentional experience and evaluate the discipline of phenomenology to the
status of science so as to ground the knowledge in "what is universally
valid,"[8] Heidegger rescued the object from the mental and conscious
domain by relocating it in a temporal and concrete mode of existence,
hence dismissing Husserl's aspiration for the universal. In Heidegger's
own terms, the project of phenomenological investigation only needs to
assume a "regional category." As a regional category, according to
Heidegger, it deals only with the temporal and local object as it shows
itself at the time of the investigation.

With phenomenological investigation being redefined as such,
Heidegger further argued the discipline does not need to impose a certain mode of being onto the object it investigates, because what shows
itself from itself is capable of giving itself a distinctive mode of presence,
encountered from "a definite manner of *looking towards them and seeing
them*."[9] Here, we can see that Heidegger had attempted to blur a long-
cherished distinction between an object-in-itself and an object-as-perceived, retained by Husserl's phenomenology as well as other modern
disciplinary studies. He argued that that distinction cannot be substantial and absolute, since a definite way of looking toward and seeing the
object is not that of something imposed upon the object, but rather
what arises from "the basis of a being-oriented regarding the objects,
and already-being-familiar with these beings."[10] The kind of familiarity
with the objects or things to be investigated is "the sedimented result of
having heard about them and having learned something about them."[11]
Heidegger thus stated that the orientation of definite ways of seeing a
certain object comes from the accumulated layers of a culture or the disciplinary tradition from which it derived its name and assumed its
mode of expression. Take the discipline of logic, for instance,

Heidegger suggested. One may never know the object of logic till one is exposed to the discipline that teaches about the certain ways of "classifying, characterizing" of the objects of consciousness and intentionality. Similarly, it is through the discipline of botany—the systematic classification and description of plants—that one comes to learn about the name and certain characteristics of a plant. Heidegger's point is clear. That is, any object to be investigated has always and already been covered up by various layers of classification, description, and naming processes of the tradition or discipline it belongs to; and it is only by going through those layers that the object is seen, encountered, and interpreted. Therefore, in a literary sense, it is hardly possible to speak of an object-in-itself *as such* or claim there is an *unmediated* access to it. It must be an illusion or a fruitless attempt, as far as Heidegger can tell, to maintain the absolute distinction between the *object-in-itself* and the *object-as-perceived*, cherished by both traditional metaphysics and the modern disciplinary studies.

To back up his argument, Heidegger returns to his example of the family table. The perceived relationship and the functionality of the table are not something external to or imposed on the table, Heidegger reminded us, but that which has been directed and oriented toward it through a shared cultural tradition that defines and classifies what a table is, where it should be located, and how it should be used. Hence, the table is both an object-in-itself and an object-as-perceived, or the thing-for-itself and the thing-for-us at the same time. It may be worthy to note here that Heidegger, with or without any awareness, has managed to separate his table from Plato's bed. One recalls, in the *Republic*, Plato had explained that the bed was only a Form or Idea. Once this Form or Idea of the bed was copied by a carpenter and turned into a material bed, it was reduced into a copy of its original; and its originality was only to be further reduced by a poet who reported his impression of the bed based on the material copy made by the carpenter.

For Heidegger, the Platonic distinction between the Form and its copies cannot continue to dominate disciplinary studies today. Should disciplinary objects and the ways of "their showing-themselves" be imbedded in that tradition of the discipline, he suggested, "this inauthenticity is no longer able to be recognized, but rather is taken to be authentic."[12] That is to say, a covered-up subject matter needs to be taken as the subject matter itself.[13] Taking a covered-up subject matter for the subject matter itself as the starting point of a phenomenological investigation, Heidegger assumes, it could lead back to a disclosure of "the history of the covering up of the subject matter," and hopefully, "get beyond the position started from and arrive at a grasp of the subject matter which is free of covering up."[14] As we can tell, Heidegger eventually transformed phenomenology into a historical enquiry that "dismantles" the tradition of a certain discipline by working regressively, as far back as possible, to uncover the layers accumulated around the objects of its investigation, or to disclose "the history of the covering up of the subject matter," only to reveal a more "primordial position" that the investigation has first started.[15] Heidegger's historical turn to uncover the disciplinary object by way of working out its "fore-having" and "fore-conception," have doubtlessly inspired the subsequent development of an ontological/historical hermeneutics, carried out by his student, Hans Gadamer.

Heidegger Devises His Own Project of Hermeneutic Investigation

Now that we have familiarized ourselves with Heidegger's critique of Husserl's phenomenology and the ways in which he made his departure from his predecessor, we are ready to explore how Heidegger devised his own project of the phenomenological investigation, which he called "the hermeneutics of facticity."

First, let us take a look at the terms that Heidegger used here to name his project. Apparently, the term "ontology" used by Heidegger does not stand merely for the study of being in the tradition of metaphysics, from which he had been trying to break away. And yet Heidegger did retain the term to acknowledge the persistent interest in the study of being in the Western intellectual tradition that "proliferates on the soil of classical Greek philosophy."[16] And he continued to use the term to indicate his own interest in identifying a particular kind of being that fits in his hermeneutic investigation. The being that Heidegger was about to identify is not the Platonic Form, or a lifeless object of consciousness and intentionality in Husserl's logical investigation, but a particular being that he named *Dasein*.

Dasein has been variously translated into the English language as "being-there," "being-in-the-world," and so on; yet, none of these terms seems to fully capture the meaning that Heidegger intended to convey here in the lecture. According to his own definition and exposition, *Dasein* is not an "object of intuition" or "the possible object of having"—possessed by a subject—but a "transitive" being—a "being-there for a while at a particular time" (i.e., "tarrying for a while," "being-there-at-home-in," and "being there-involved-in").[17] As such, *Dasein* is a being-in-the-world, capable of being with itself (at-home-in), as well as with others (there-involved-in), for a period of temporal/spatial duration. *Dasein* is not a static and constant presence, but it is always on the move and in the stage of being "wakeful," to "be-on-the-way" to and from itself.[18] As such, *Dasein* indeed has a life of its own, which Heidegger called "factical." In Heidegger's explanation, *Dasein* in a stage of being factical means that it is "the being-there of *Dasein* in the awhileness of temporal particularity."[19] Therefore, for Heidegger, his ontology is the investigation of *Dasein*'s factical life as a particular being in its temporal modality, which he termed the "hermeneutics of facticity."

Here, we can already tell that Heidegger was about to introduce a fundamental change into the disciplines of not only ontology but of hermeneutics, by replacing the objects of the disciplinary investigation from a constant and hence *static* presence to a *moving* being that is transitory and temporal by nature.

Leaving the discipline of ontology aside, we shall only focus on how Heidegger had radically transformed the nature and practice of hermeneutics by following him through a detour into the history of the discipline that had defined and redefined the scope of its investigation from antiquity to the present. According to Heidegger, with Plato, hermeneutic activity was simply viewed as an "announcing and making known" of what had previously existed but was perceived as obscured or concealed at the time of investigation. Thus, hermeneutics in the Greek understanding was not intended to discover or find something new, but to uncover or reveal what had been already there. It was much less "vigorous" than the later tradition of biblical exegesis, Heidegger pointed out. However, in the hands of St. Augustine, hermeneutics was transformed into a "doctrine of interpretation," intended to guide man's approach to the "ambiguous passages in Scriptures," with certain provisions such as "the fear of God," and "the sole care of seeking God's will in Scriptures." In the nineteenth century, the term was reappropriated by Schleiermacher and Dilthey to refer to "an art or technique of understanding" of historical consciousness and "the formulation for rules of understanding" of written texts of the past traditions.[20]

Whereas both classical and modern hermeneutic traditions were intended to define objects for disciplinary investigation as metaphysical constant such as God's will in the Scriptures and historical consciousness in the written texts, Heidegger's new hermeneutics freed itself from doctrinal restraint imposed by St. Augustine and scientific and technical framework assigned by the modern theologians and historians by choosing a temporal and transitive being in its particular mode of being in the world as the object of the disciplinary investigation.

Now the issue for Heidegger is to demonstrate how to carry out the hermeneutic project of investigation of such a moving object and what textual strategies are needed to apply to the procedure of investigation.

First of all, Heidegger calls attention to the fact that, as a temporal and transient being, *Dasein* has a fore-structure or potentiality to express itself in advance and propel itself forward and the capability of articulating itself "with respect to, on the basis of, and with a view to" its factical character of being.[21]

To illustrate his statement about the fore-structure of *Dasein*, Heidegger continues to use the example of his family table. First, he tells us, the table in his family room is a specific mode of *Dasein* being-there in the world. Standing in its particular temporal/spatial mode, the table has always and already the potentiality to be there as such with respect to, on the basis of, with a view to its transitive and temporal nature. That is to say, Heidegger stated, the table, as a particular mode of *Dasein* in its temporal particularity, has already and always a "view to developing in it a radical wakefulness for itself," as it is "hermeneutically interrogated with respect to and on the basis of the character of its being."[22]

Heidegger's last statement seems to tempt us to make a hasty suggestion here. That is, it may be the hermeneutical interrogation that draws out the potential tendency of *Dasein* to propel itself forward and express itself. Yet, Heidegger's distinction of the notions of "mutually dependent" from "mutually belonging" seems to discourage us to draw such a conclusion. The distinction appears to be important here. The first notion may refer to a situation where the two entities are originally independent from each other, but come to form a relation as a certain condition occurs, such as a commodity that happens to satisfy a market and hence forms a supply-and-demand relation with it; the second notion indicates an inherent bond between the two entities regardless of any external conditions, or even two different aspects of the same entities. For Heidegger, the tendency of *Dasein* to propel itself forward as a specific mode of being-there, and the hermeneutic interpretation of such a mode of being-there are mutually belonging together; in fact, they are the two co-relating aspects of *Dasein*'s own factical life. In his words, the hermeneutic interpretation is "a being which belongs to the being factical life itself," and it is a distinctive mode of "how the character of being of facticity *is*."[23] As such, the ontological gap between the hermeneutic interpretation and the factical life of *Dasein* is closed, and so is the epistemological division of a perceiving subject and a perceived object.

Given hermeneutic interpretation and the *Dasein*'s factical life are the co-relating aspects of *Dasein* itself, Heidegger thus suggested that to interpret *Dasein hermeneutically* is to take sides with its "presumed mode of access."[24] Taking sides with *Dasein*'s mode of access enables the possibility of gaining insight into the life of the transitive being—how it shows itself as "something capable of interpretation and in need of interpretation and in some state of having-been-interpreted."[25] Further, it gives a sense of the manner and timing in which "in *what way and when* our *Dasein* calls for this kind of interpretation."[26] For Heidegger, taking sides with *Dasein* and seeing it from its presumed mode of access, and thereby gaining a sense of when the interpretation is called for, is both ontologically and epistemologically possible, because *Dasein* and the hermeneutical interpretation of its temporal and transitory mode of being-there belong to one another.

We noticed here that in his layout of the project of hermeneutic investigation there is no place for an intentional or conscious subject who is doing the engaging, grasping, and approaching of the factical life of *Dasein*. Heidegger simply stated that to investigate is to take sides with the presumed mode of access of *Dasein*, which is "our own." However, to say that *Dasein* in each case is our own, does not amount to a suggestion that "we," as human *Dasein*s, possess *Dasien* as an object of investigation and interpretation. In fact, the term "we," may not necessarily refer to human subjects; but broadly conceived, refers to the faceless and nameless beings that are capable of assuming a temporal mode of being-there, of becoming themselves and of interpreting themselves. As far as Heidegger is concerned, man, at most, is a constitutive part of *Dasein* in its temporal mode of being and becoming, and hence, has some access to the former, that is, seeing from the side of *Dasein* and knowing how it is to be there in the world in a specific mode at a particular time.

Let us summarize what Heidegger was proposing here. Defined negatively, hermeneutics is no longer "a doctrine about the conditions, the objects, the means, and the communication and practical application of interpretation."[27] Since what is being encountered is not a static presence or lifeless object but a moving being in the world, assuming a temporal and particular mode of existence of becoming, the hermeneutic interpretation cannot take "cognizance of something" by "having knowledge about it,"[28] or mastery of the formulas for understanding what is constant and formal. Without claiming a universal knowledge of what is external, constant, and hence formal, Heidegger's ontological hermeneutics directs attention to "the definite and decisive possibility of concrete facility" of *Dasein's* temporal and particular mode of becoming—being wakeful.[29] Hence, defined positively, Heidegger's ontological hermeneutics is an investigation of a temporal and particular being and its modes of existence in the world on its way to "being-wakeful," not looking from the opposite side or at distance from it, but taking its own side; in other words, it is a self-interpretation of its own temporal particularity as a being in the world or on the way to becoming.

Ultimately, Heidegger wants to explore a model of investigation of the phenomenal without depending on either a metaphysical presence who originates its movement and assigns its designation, a human interpretive subject who sees and interprets its motion and modality from an objective distance, or an object, ready-at-hand, to be seen, investigated, and objectified. Without relying on the traditional subject-object conceptual schema, what Heidegger's ontological hermeneutics promises here is the opening of a horizon of mutual encounter between the various aspects of *Dasein's* factical life itself, such as its tendency to propel, and the capability to assume different modes of existence for a while at a given time. The mutual encounter between *Dasein's* various aspects of being-there in-the-world appears to be entirely possible because *Dasein* has a factical life and the hermeneutic interpretation "belongs to the being of factical life itself."[30]

Heidegger's Ontological Hermeneutic Worldview Compared with a Buddhist Outlook

Heidegger's ontological hermeneutics, among other things, introduces a radically different worldview than that presented in mainstream conceptual systems in the West. First, it looks at the world of phenomena as the movement of temporal beings in the world, appearing in its various modes of becoming and existence without a metaphysical presence as the originating point, or the primary cause. Second, it sees the operation of such a phenomenal world without a rational or transcendental subject, being either divine or human, to carry out that cause and interpret its meaning. And third, if such a worldview dismissed an originator or a subject, it does not have any need for an object, perceived as something ready-at-hand, being subjected to the processes of investigation and objectification.

Such a radical worldview poses a serious challenge to various time-honored conceptual systems and traditions and some of their most important metaphysical notions, such as Plato's Form, Aristotle's substance, Augustine's God, Descartes's subject, Hegel's spirit, Husserl's conscious intention—to name only a few. In those systems, a theo-metaphysical presence was usually identified as the ultimate cause in determining the unfolding process and the meaning of world events and movement. Heidegger did not intend in his lecture to prove or disprove whether there had been a metaphysical origin that engenders a phenomenal world and hence the necessity of retaining an ontological distinction between Being and beings, and presence and the present things. He simply reminded his audience that such traditional Western metaphysical worldviews may be shaped and conditioned by a historical mistake, a misconception and misinterpretation of the notion of being. He explained that in the early Greek understanding, "being" was linked with the verb "to be." Yet, during the course of time, that link was lost and the word became a noun. The change from verb to noun reduces "being" to a constant and hence static presence, based on which, the subsequent Western metaphysics and theology developed and flourished. Heidegger believed that the development of the systems of theo-metaphysics had systematically concealed the original meaning of "being" as a temporal and transitive reality, with various temporal modes of expression and existence in the world. The project that he devised in the lecture called the "facticity of *Dasein*" was intended to rectify this important conceptual error by attempting to recover the primordial meaning of being as a temporal and transitive movement. Heidegger's project, needless to say, has inspired a number of post-metaphysical projects of deconstruction to be carried out by thinkers such as Derrida, Foucault, Habermas, Rorty, and others.

The worldview implied by Heidegger's ontological hermeneutics certainly brings out a parallel to the Buddhist outlook of the world. A Buddhist view of the world as being co-originated and dependent, arising without a theo-metaphysical origin or inherent nature—Brahma or Atman—can be traced back to Sakyamuni's own enlightenment experiences, in which he sees with his own enlightened eyes, the arising of the co-originating and mutually dependent matter/events (dharmas) that constituted his past lives, without an originating point or a primary cause. It is this very seeing experience of the Buddha that had constituted the doctrinal foundation of Dependent Co-Origination. Since the Buddha's time, there had been persistent efforts to undermine and deconstruct a theo-metaphysical presence throughout the Buddhist history of interpretation, attempting to explain the world as a *concurrent* happening of physical and psychological events, without relying on a metaphysical entity, as a radical alternative to metaphysical thinking of origin as a constant presence. Also, different generations of interpreters employed different languages and metaphors to explain how the co-dependently originated world could never be grasped by any viewing and knowing subjects from a single vantage point. The Buddha's teaching of No-Self, which is also derived from the imagery revealed to him in the watch of his Enlightenment, tells us that there is no inherent and permanent self-nature in what was perceived as a human being, in fact, is composite, transitive, and temporal. The disappearance of a subject and hence a subjective viewpoint leads to the dissolving of the subject-object schema that separates the world into the binary pairs of substance and appearance, *object-in-itself* and *object-as-perceived*.

Heidegger also regarded that a world without a theo-metaphysical presence is also absent of a subject. Since there is no theo-metaphysical origin in his world picture, there is no need for a human subject as an acting and representative agent of that originating force or the primary cause. Against the main Western theo-metaphysical traditions that treat a human subject as one endowed with divinity or reason, and hence associated with the conscious ego and so on, Heidegger claimed that he wants to propose a new way of thinking of the human subject that is not associated with "the ideas of 'ego,' person, ego-pole, center of act." As he specified, "the concept of the self is . . . not to be taken as something having its origin in an 'ego,' in terms of having intention."[31]

Heidegger did not discuss an alternative view of man in the lecture. Considered from a general framework of his onto-hermeneutic view, we may suggest that Heidegger would grant that man is at best a constitutive part of *Dasein*, as it assumes the temporal mode of being there in the world at a particular time. Man is a human *Dasein* only as he partakes in the temporal and particular mode of existence and expression of *Dasein*. Yet, since *Dasein* is not a transcendent being such as a god or spirit who creates and defines man's being and existence, but is itself a temporal being in the world, a human *Dasein* assumes its identity only through partaking of *Dasien*'s own temporal particularity. The temporality and composite nature of man is rather similar to the Buddha's teaching of man as the temporal grouping of the five aggregates—a series of temporal physical and psychological acts or events that both form a condition of his past lives and projects into his future. Man is a man only when he becomes a temporal locus of these acts or events, which denies a strong religious conviction that there is a "self" that survives the temporal particularity of the aggregates, or an inherent and unchanging self-nature that is behind or beyond the composite groupings.

On the Western front, Heidegger's attempt to do away with the notion of man as a conscious being, ego-pole, and center of action, needless to say, anticipated what Foucault claimed as "the death of man." Foucault discovered that in the rise of modernity and the modern disciplinary studies of natural, social, and human sciences, man as the subject is eventually replaced by the intricate, endless, and back-and-forth power play with these disciplinary practices and the context of modernity in general. Echoing Nietzsche's outcry that "God is dead," both Heidegger and Foucault saw an essential connection between the two primary events of associated disappearances. That is, if God and man mutually presuppose and belong to one another, the death of one naturally leads to the other.

If there is no perceived need for a subject, divine or rational, there will be no need for an object either. For Heidegger, an object in the modern disciplinary studies is usually perceived as something out there, available and ready-at-hand to be investigated, classified, and objectified by a subject for a larger purpose. In his onto-hermeneutic world, what is being observed and investigated is not an object in that sense, because it cannot be grasped by a subject as "an isolating contrast," but "a being that belongs to the being of factical life itself."[32]

Heidegger's Table and Fa-tsang's Golden Lions

To further compare Heidegger's onto-hermeneutic worldview with that of the Buddhist, we may want to examine the ways in which each interprets the world as a moving reality without a metaphysical origin and a subject-object schema. There are two convenient examples that we can take a look at. One is Heidegger's analysis of his family table that he continued to use throughout his lecture; and the other is a Buddhist narrative account of a pair of golden lions, used to illustrate the doctrine of Dependent Co-Origination of world phenomena.

In Heidegger's analysis, when approaching the table, one does not need to speculate on where and how the table in his family room first comes from and goes into existence, nor treating it as a copy or derivative of some primary concept of the table. It is only a piece of furniture, a material thing in space, here and now, standing face-to-face with the one who approaches it. There is no way to define its nature independent from its other attributes and qualities either. For the table is at once a thing of *nature*, made of wood or stone, and a thing of *value*, it is beautiful. The thing of nature and the thing of value are not separable, since "the latter always contains the being of a natural thing as the basic stratum."[33] Therefore, for Heidegger, the table *simultaneously* displays its perceived nature (of being wood or metal), the sentimental and aesthetic values (of being passed down by the grandparents and being beautiful), as well as its everyday functionality (to sew, play, and write on). All these inherent and perceived attributes of the table, as Heidegger put it, come to the fore as it was approached, utilized, and interpreted by the specific family members at a particular time.

To restrict his analysis to the phenomenological level—to the thing that is already in existence available, here and now—Heidegger discouraged the speculation of what is beyond or behind the thing itself and the breaking down of its nature, value, and functionality into analytical categories. Heidegger's phenomenological treatment strongly resembles the Buddhist hermeneutic strategies employed by a monk to interpret how world phenomena do not originate from temporal beings, but rise independently with each other—the doctrine of Dependent Co-Origination.

From a well-known text, "Treatise on the Golden Lion," composed in the seventh century China,[34] we learned that the occasion that initiated the eminent monk Fa-tsang's teaching was the invitation extended to him by Empress Wu to come to the palace to explain the Buddhist doctrine of Emptiness. Fa-tsang's interpretative strategies were *hermeneutical*, in that he started out with concrete and visible phenomena and engaged them with what is abstract and distant. To state that everything is devoid of a self-nature and thus empty, the monk used the golden lions standing in front of the palace as an example. First, he pointed out that the gold the golden lions are made of is without a self-nature, and hence empty, so that craftsmen could, depending on the perceived need and tools available, craft it into anything. Yet, this empty nature of the gold is not something that is beyond or behind the golden lions that it was shaped into, but appears as such only as the gold was melted and reshaped into a pair of golden lions. Thus, Fa-tsang explains, the perceived nature of gold arises dependently, or in relationship with the golden lions—as the gold took a material form. That is, the empty nature of the gold and the golden lions co-originate from or arise in dependence of each other. Both being of gold, neither has an inherent self-nature. Thus, it follows, the golden lions are not a copy of the gold, but they are gold themselves. Although the gold and golden lions are different in form and perhaps in value and functionality, the monk continued, they are not *fundamentally* different from each other in nature—empty and co-originating—and hence, there is no need to retain an absolute distinction between them.

Cross-Cultural Encounter as the Movement of World Encounter

Heidegger had maintained this onto-hermeneutic worldview developed in the lecture in the 1920s and used it to explain various modern phenomena. For instance, as we have discussed in previous chapters, Heidegger dismissed the metalinguistic view of language as a system of written and spoken signs invented by human speaking subjects for a practical purpose and proposed a cosmic model of language that treats it as the flowering of the mouth, through which the earth blossoms toward that of the sky. In his analysis of modern technology, Heidegger managed to demonstrate how the modern technological world operates without an originating point or a subject-object schema. As a way of setting up the world, it is neither "objective" nor "subjective," in the usual sense that man designs and applies a tool to an object. Rather, it became an "automatic" process of setting up and bringing together the world phenomena in which man, machines, and objects are no longer separable.

Interestingly, the parallel between Heidegger and the Buddhist onto-hermeneutic worldviews was rather recently discovered and articulated by the scientific community. Scientists came to an appreciation of Heidegger's analysis of the scientific and technological world through the detour into and encounter with the traditions of Eastern mysticism.[35] Research physicist and author of *The Tao of Physics*, Fritjof Capra pointed out that the Eastern mystical worldviews preserved in Hinduism, Buddhism, and Taoism had actually anticipated and hence provided a theoretical foundation for modern physical science. For instance, modern quantum physicists find a strong parallel in Eastern mysticism, in seeing the physical universe as "inseparable reality—forever in motion, alive, organic; spiritual and material at the same time." The reason for this is simple. In structured scientific observation, objects displayed "a fluid and ever-changing character," therefore, the "division of nature into separate objects" can not be fundamental."[36] Changing views of the physical universe and the disciplinary practice of New Physics have also transformed the consciousness and outlook of the world of the physicists themselves. Questions and challenges were posed to the Copenhagen Theory, which had divided the world into two systems: the observed system—objects to be observed and investigated—and the observing system—the research apparatuses and the intention and objectives of the human observers. The New Physics community became increasingly aware that in the actual process of scientific research the distinction cannot always be retained, because "the observing system is described in operational terms" that "permit scientists to set up and carry out their experiments." The truth of the matter is that "the measuring devices and the scientists are effectively joined into one complex system which has no distinct, well-defined parts, and the experimental apparatus does not have to be described as an isolated physical entity."[37] Capra's attempt to establish a paradigm for not only speculating upon the possible wider religious and metaphysical influence on the new physical science, but dialogues between the East and West, tradition and modernity have attained immerse popularity, according to John Clarke. In his recent work, *The Tao of the West*, Clarke observed that Capra's attempt to develop an alternative conceptual framework to that of the mechanistic, dualistic, and rationalistic one put forward by Galileo and Descartes has a great appeal for a large following who were searching for a holistic worldview that could accommodate both religion and spirituality, science and technology.[38]

Given that there have been decades of exposure in the West to both Heidegger's onto-hermeneutical and Eastern mystical worldviews such as the Buddhist view of the world as co-dependently arising, it may be the time to attempt to outline an alternative cross-cultural hermeneutics or perhaps a new worldview that perceives the encounter of the different cultural traditions without depending on transcendental a prioris, assuming the notions of origin, genealogy, race, boundary, and Otherness, or a timeless being to reside over and above the movement of the encounter, predetermining its course and unfolding process.

Suspending a metaphysical a priori will perhaps assist us in deconstructing an epistemological dualism dividing the world into subject and object, self and other, insider and outsider, which has per-

petuated and sustained an East-West binarism that continues to dominate the comparative studies of philosophies and religions in the academy and a cross-cultural understanding in the public arena. Such
dualistic review and treatment not only obstructed the emergence of
the cross-cultural encounter as a world movement, but also concealed
the individual and concrete mode of formation and transformation of
those world events as they appeared in the world, each with its own
temporal particularity.

To put the metaphysical given and epistemological dualism on
hold, we may begin to see that various instances of the East-West
encounter are not conceived in a metaphysical notion *inhere* in a metaphysical presence, but *adhere* and *cohere* with one another and with
other series of political, cultural, and social events, either preceding or
concurrent with them. For example, the instances in the dialogue
between Heidegger and his Japanese visitor in the first part of the twentieth century, and the meeting between Rorty and Balslev in the second
part of the century, did not originate from an a priori but co-dependently arose in relationship to or against their respective historical and
contemporary social, political, and cultural events.

In his lecture, Heidegger stressed that "there is no generality in
hermeneutical understanding over and above what is formal,"[39] and
that "what is being encountered" is the "multiplicity of cultures which
are in themselves ontically on a par with each other," and it is the "morphological observation" that differentiates them from each other.[40]
Should the multiplicity of cultures be allowed to re-emerge, Heidegger
seemed to imply, we may need to "reverse" the morphological observation in order to break down the binary categories used in the observation such as that of the familiar and unfamiliar.

Heidegger first pointed out that what appears to be unfamiliar is
not derived from a preconceived notion or metaphysical concept or a
formal structure. The unfamiliar appears to be so only when it is being
looked at and seen as such from a particular viewpoint at a particular
time. Yet, the very *looking toward* and seeing the unfamiliar has always
and already been oriented by the knowledge of a familiarity with it—
having heard and read about it, or developed an interest in or preju-
dice against it. Thus this *looking toward*, in Heidegger's term, is "the
directional seeing" that had taken place prior to the actual encounter
with the unfamiliar—it has already borne a relation with the latter.
Hence, Heidegger suggested, the unfamiliar comes with "a reference
of familiarity" and it "signifies and points itself" to "a peculiar context

of reference."[41] If the unfamiliar is already embedded in the familiar, and "within the initial givens...which are closest to us," at a particular time, the lack of familiarity—the unfamiliarity, is only a form of "inexplicit familiarity." Thus perceived, the familiar and unfamiliar are two "comparative" terms rather than binary opposites.[42]

The mutual embeddedness and eventual identification of what is familiar and unfamiliar, reminiscent of the gold and the golden lions of the Buddhist narrative, helps us here to refocus and examine the category of the foreign, prevailing in all the instances of structured observation and investigation of the cross-cultural encounter. Heidegger and Fa-tsang help us to realize that in every instance of an encounter, there will be nothing that is originally or purely foreign to meet for the first time. Hence, when we refer to something as if it was foreign and strange and that it "stands in the way" and appears to be "disturbing," we realize that the impressions and characterizations of it "belong to the very temporality of the world's being-encountered," as Heidegger put it; and it is in this movement of world encounter that the foreignness and strangeness is "shaken up and awakened," and the sense of being different is heightened. However, the sense of the discomfort and disturbance in the moment of encounter with the foreign and strange does not need to be overcome. For when "familiarity is disturbed" and has appeared so in its disturbed stage, it gives rise to "the contingent otherwise than one thought."[43]

Heidegger continued to pursue this line of thinking thirty years after he gave the lecture. In his Dialogue with the Japanese visitor, he carried on the conversation of the notion of the mutual embeddedness of familiarity and unfamiliarity in the cross-cultural context. Heidegger related to his visitor that the reason we are able to reach an understanding of what is "originally familiar" is because we do not avoid "things strange to us."[44] For what is "originally familiar" is what "has been entrusted to our nature," which becomes part of our being. However, feeling at home with the original familiarity that was entrusted to us only surfaces "at the last," and only when what was "foreign" presents itself to our very eye.[45] Therefore, Heidegger concluded, every time we intend for nearness, remoteness comes to the fore; and everywhere we run into the "the nearest nearness which we constantly rush ahead of," it "strikes us strange each time anew when we catch sight of it."[46]

To make sense of this seemingly strange circularity in the onto-hermeneutic world, as we discussed in previous chapters, Heidegger had pointed out that the notion of linear time is inadequate to grasp the movement of the face-to-face encounter; because, in the succession of the "nows," what comes after the "now" and what comes before "are closed off from each other."[47] Moreover, Heidegger pointed out, not only did we need to breakdown the binary categories used in the usual structured observation and hermeneutic investigation, but also we need to deconstruct the conventional social conception and measurement of space and time. For instance, the usual temporal and spatial parameters of physical distance, such as that of near and far, are apparently inadequate to designate the movement of the world encounter, to which, instances of the cross-cultural meeting are its constituents. Heidegger argued the notions of the near or far do not merely refer to a "spatial-temporal relation" to be measured in terms of "space and time considered as parameters,"[48] but manifestation of "the motion in which the world's regions face each other."[49] In Heidegger's view, it is only when we can conceptualize time and space, not as static temporal/spatial presence, but as moving in their "cyclical" motion, that the encounter of the world's regions takes place. Such a movement of the world encounter would perhaps only occur in Heidegger's world picture of the fourfold, which consists of "the gods and mortals and the sky and earth," with each standing in "a certain contrast to" the other "as different magnitudes of our distance from objects."[50] Could Heidegger's world picture as the dynamic movement and mutual encounter of fourfold beings—gods, mortals, heaven, and earth—derived from an ancient Greek picture of the cosmos, inspire a future world picture? Could different beings stand "face-to-face with one another," in a perpetual motion and movement—not only that of the familiar and near, or one's self, but the unfamiliar and far, or one's Other? Heidegger seems to think so. He predicts, when this prevails, "all things are open to one another in their self-concealment; thus one extends itself to the other, and thus all remain themselves; one is over the other as its guardian watching over the other, over it as its veil"—as Heidegger gently reminds us.[51]

NOTES

Introduction

1. Smith made his remark in the introduction to his new edition of *World's Religions* (San Francisco, Harper, 1991), Rorty commented on the topic after attending the Sixth East–West Philosophy Conference at the University of Hawaii in 1989. See Anindita N. Balslev's letter to Rorty, in Balslev, ed., *Cultural Otherness* (Atlanta: Scholars Press, 1991), 31.

2. Clarke quoted Goethe's and Kipling's sayings at the beginning of his book, *Oriental Enlightenment* (New York: Routledge, 1997).

3. See Jerry H. Bentley's *Old World Encounters*; Mary B. Cambell's *The Witness and the Other World*; and Stuart B. Schwartz's edited volume, *Implicit Understanding*.

4. Mary Campbell, *The Witness and the Other World: Exotic European Travel Writing, 400–1600* (Ithaca: Cornell University Press, 1988), 3.

5. Ibid., 7.

6. Ibid., 8.

7. Ibid., 9.

8. See Clarke's discussion in his introduction to *Oriental Enlightenment*.

9. See Rorty's letter to Balslev in *Cultural Otherness*. 67–68.

1. The Question of Legitimacy of Comparative Philosophy

1. See "Proceedings for the International Symposium on Rorty, Pragmatism and Chinese Philosophy"—July 17–18, 2004, published by East China Normal University, Shanghai, China.

2. Anindita N. Balslev, ed., *Cultural Otherness: Correspondence with Richard Rorty* (Atlanta: Scholars Press, 1991), 59. *Cultural Otherness*.

3. Ibid., 21.

4. Ibid., 31.

5. Ibid., 79.

6. See Balslev's argument in the preface to *Cultural Otherness.*

7. *Cultural Otherness*, 104.

8. Ibid., 112.

9. Rorty's conference paper, "Philosophers, Novelists, and Intercultural Comparison," published as an appendix in *Cultural Otherness,* 113.

10. *Cultural Otherness*, 107.

11. Ibid., 110.

12. Ibid., 105.

13. Ibid., 59.

14. See Rorty's discussion of whether Asians need philosophy in his book review of Larson and Deutsch's edited book, *New Essays in Comparative Philosophy,* quoted in Balslev's letter to Rorty, included in *Cultural Otherness,* 59.

15. *Cultural Otherness*, 59.

16. Ibid., 68.

17. Ibid., 112.

18. Ibid., 113.

19. Ibid., 114.

20. Ibid, 113.

21. Ibid., 51.

22. Ibid., 32.

23. See Rorty's comparison of Heidegger and Dewey in his essay "Overcoming Tradition" in *Consequences of Pragmatism* (Minneapolis: University of Minnesota Press, 1982).

24. *Cultural Otherness*, 13.

25. Ibid., 22.

26. Ibid., 47.

27. Ibid., 11.

28. Ibid., 10–11.

29. Ibid., 80.

30. Ibid., 79.

31. Ibid., 81.

32. Ibid., 10.

33. Ibid., 15.

34. Ibid., 76.

35. See Balslev's preface to *Cultural Otherness.* 21.

36. *Cultural Otherness.* 89.

37. Ibid., 89.

38. Ibid., 89.

39. Ibid., 60.

40. Ibid., 90.

41. Ibid., 61.

42. Ibid., 39.

43. Ibid., 42.

44. Ibid, 42.

45. Ibid., 11.

46. See Balslev's preface to *Cultural Otherness.* 17.

Chapter 2. Philosophy and Cultural Otherness

1. See Rorty's argument in his "Keeping Philosophy Pure: An Essay on Wittgenstein," in *Consequences of Pragmatism* (Minneapolis, University of Minnesota Press, 1982).

2. *Cultural Otherness.* 67.

3. Ibid., 98.

4. Rorty, *Consequence of Pragmatism.* 173.

5. *Cultural Otherness.* 67.

6. Ibid., 67–68.

7. Ibid., 67.

8. *Consequences of Pragmatism*, 57.

9. See Rorty's discussion of the topic in his *Philosophy and the Mirror of Nature* (Princeton, Princeton University Press, 1979). 378.

10. Rorty, introduction to *Consequences of Pragmatism*. xi.

11. Rorty, *Philosophy and the Mirror of Nature*. 378.

12. Ibid., 152–53.

13. See Georgia Warnke's comments on Rorty in her *Gadamer— Hermeneutics, Tradition and Reason* (Stanford, Stanford University Press, 1987), 153.

14. Ibid., 152.

15. Rorty, *Consequences of Pragmatism*. 173.

16. Quoted from Warnke, 153.

17. Ibid., 151––52.

18. See Rorty's essay, "Habermas and Lyotard on Postmodernity," in *Habermas and Modernity*, ed. Richard J. Bernstein (Massachusetts, MIT Press, 1994), 166.

19. Rorty's remarks quoted in Warnke, 154.

20. Ibid., 152.

21. Ibid., 154.

22. Ibid., 154.

23. *Cultural Otherness*. 26-27.

24. Ibid., 11.

25. Ibid., 26.

26. Ibid., 10.

27. Ibid., 121.

28. Lars-Henrik Schmidt, "Commonness across Cultures" in *Cross-Cultural Conversation*, ed. Anindita N. Balselv (Atlanta, Scholars Press, 1996), 121.

29. Ibid., 122.

30. Ibid., 122.

31. Quoted from Don Howard's "The History That We Are" in *Cross-Cultural Conversation*, 52.

32. Ibid., 55–56

33. Quoted from *Cultural Otherness.* 58.

34. Howard, 45–49.

35. Ibid., 47.

36. Ibid., 47.

37. See William Desmond's introduction to *Desire, Dialectics and Otherness* (New Haven, Yale University Press, 1987).

38. Schmidt, 122.

39. *Cultural Otherness.* 39.

40. Ibid., 39.

41. Ibid., 98.

42. Ibid., 40.

43. Ibid., 40.

44. Ibid., 97–98.

45. Ibid., 92–93.

46. Ibid., 41.

47. Ibid., 40–41.

48. Ibid., 77.

49. Ibid., 77.

50. James Clifford, *The Predicament of Culture: 20th Century Ethnography, Literature, and Art* (Cambridge, Massachusetts, Harvard University Press, 1988), 262–63.

51. Ibid., 256.

52. Ibid., 256.

53. Rey Chow, *Writing Diaspora: Tactics of Intervention in Contemporary Cultural Studies* (Bloomington: Indiana University Press, 1993), 40.

54. Ibid., 42–43.

55. Ibid., 42.

56. Ibid., 37.

57. Ibid., 36.

58. There are more discussions encouraging the native remain silent as a form of resistance to the post-colonial perpetuation of colonial representation of indigenous peoples in Said's "How Anthropology Makes Its Interlocutors" and James Scott's *Weapons of the Weak* as well as Rey Chow's *Writing Diaspora*.

59. Edward Said, "How Anthropology Makes Its Interlocutors," *Critical Enquiry* Winter, 1989, (Minneapolis, University of Minnesota Press), 200.

60. Ibid., 121.

Chapter 3. On the Way to a "Common" Language

1. *Heidegger and Asian Thought*, ed. Graham Parkes (Honolulu, University of Hawaii Press, 1987), 7.

2. See the discussion of various instances of Heidegger's meeting with Eastern thinkers by his students and commentators in *Heidegger and Asian Thought*.

3. See the articles by Heidegger's student Otto Poggeler, "West-East Dialogue: Heidegger and Lao-tzu" and his English translator Joan Stambaugh's, "Heidegger, Taoism and the Question of Metaphysics," in *Heidegger and Asian Thought*.

4. *Heidegger and Asian Thought*. 13.

5. "A Dialogue on Language," in *On the Way to Language*. 2.

6. Ibid., 4.

7. Ibid., 3.

8. Ibid., 5.

9. In *Martin Heidegger: Basic Writings*, ed. by David Farrell Krell (New York: Harper & Row, 1977), 213.

10. "The Nature of Language," in *On the Way to Language*, 75.

11. Ibid., 76.

12. Heidegger, quoted from Hubert L. Dreyfus's *Being-in-the-World* (Massachusetts, MIT Press, 1994), 216–18.

13. "The Nature of Language," 58.

14. "A Dialogue on Language," 5.

15. Ibid., 8.

16. Ibid., 8.

17. Ibid., 23.

18. Ibid., 23

19. Ibid., 45.

20. Heidegger, "The Thinker as Poet," in *Poetry, Language, Thought*, trans., Albert Hofstadter (New York: Harper & Row, 1971), 13.

21. "A Dialogue on Language," 44–45.

22. Ibid., 46.

23. Ibid., 44.

24. Ibid., 45.

25. Ibid., 44.

26. Ibid., 45.

27. Ibid., 45.

28. David Kolb, *The Critique of Pure Modernity* (Chicago: University of Chicago Press, 1986), 159.

29. "A Dialogue on Language," 47.

30. Ibid., 47.

31. Ibid., 47.

32. Ibid., 46.

33. "The Nature of Language," 81.

34. "A Dialogue on Language," 47.

35. Parkes, "Afterwards" in *Heidegger and Asian Thought.* 216.

36. "A Dialogue on Language,"41.

37. Ibid., 19.

38. Ibid., 41.

39. "The Nature of Language," 99.

40. Ibid., 98.

41. *Yiang* here assumes the simplified form.

42. Ibid., 98.

43. Ibid., 98–99.

44. Ibid., 107.

45. Quoted from Dreyfus's *Being-in-the-World*, 219.

46. Ibid., 221.

47. "A Dialogue on Language," 53.

Chapter 4. On the Way to a Cross-Cultural Hermeneutics

1. "A Dialogue on Language," 13.

2. Ibid., 29.

3. Ibid., 29.

4. "The Nature of Language," in *On the Way to Language*, 74.

5. "A Dialogue on Language," 28.

6. Ibid., 11.

7. Ibid., 30.

8. Ibid., 30

9. Ibid., 40.

10. Ibid., 32.

11. "The Nature of Language," 83.

12. See David Kolb's discussion of Heidegger's position on the East-West relation in his *The Critique of Pure Modernity* (Chicago, University of Chicago Press, 1986), 163.

13. Ibid., 161.

14. "A Dialogue on Language," 40.

15. Ibid., 40.

16. Ibid., 51.

17. "The Nature of Language," 106.

18. *Being and Time*, 148. Quoted from Kohei Mizoguchi's "Heidegger's Bremen Lectures" in Parkes's edited, *Heidegger and Asian Thought* (Honolulu: University of Hawaii Press, 1987), 196–97.

19. "The Nature of Language," 104.

20. "A Dialogue on Language," 53.

21. See Heidegger, *Identity and Difference* 103/36, quoted from Kolb's *The Critique of Pure Modernity*. 159.

22. Kolb, *The Critique of Pure Modernity*. 231.

23. Ibid., 232.

24. Ibid., 234.

25. See Yasuo Yuasa's discussion of this period of history in his "The Encounter of Modern Japanese Philosophy with Heidegger," in *Heidegger and Asian Thought*. 156.

26. Kolb's *The Critique of Pure Modernity*. 233.

27. Ibid., 232.

28. Ibid., 232.

29. Ibid., 233.

30. Ibid., 233

31. "A Dialogue on Language," 2.

32. Ibid., 15.

33. Ibid., 2.

34. Ibid., 18.

35. Ibid., 18.

36. Ibid., 17.

37. Ibid., 17.

38. Ibid., 17.

39. Ibid., 17.

40. See Kohei Mizoguchi's discussion of Heidegger's position in his comments on Heidegger's Bremen lectures, in *Heidegger and Asian Thought*. 187–98.

41. Ibid., 191.

42. Ibid., 190–91.

43. Ibid., 190.

44. Ibid., 190.

45. David M. Levin, "Mudra as Thinking," in *Heidegger and Asian Thought*. 245.

46. See both articles "Mudra as Thinking" and "Heidegger's Way with Sinitic Thinking," in *Heidegger and Asian Thought*.

47. Levin's "Mudra as Thinking," in *Heidegger and Asian Thought*. 246.

48. Guenther, "Indian Buddhist Thought in Tibetan Perspective," in *Tibetan Buddhism in Western Perspective*, 115–38, quoted by Levin in his "Mudra as Thinking," 264.

49. D. T. Suzuki, *Essays in Zen Buddhism* (New York, Grove Press, 1961), 234, quoted from Levin's "Mudra as Thinking," 256.

50. "A Dialogue on Language," 18–19.

51. Quoted from Levin's "Mudra as Thinking," 248.

52. Akihiro Takeichi, "On the Origin of Nihilism," in *Heidegger and Asian Thought*. 182–83.

53. Ibid., 185.

54. "The Question Concerning Technology," in *Martin Heidegger: Basic Writings*, edited by David Farrell Krell (New York, Harper & Row, 1977), 307.

55. Ibid.,17–18/18–19.

56. Kolb, *The Critique of Pure Modernity*. 155.

Chapter 5. Heidegger's Ontological Hermeneutics as a Worldview and World Encounter

1. Heidegger, *Ontology—The Hermeneutics of Facticity*, 17. Hereafter cited as *Ontology*.

2. Ibid., 56.

3. Ibid., 55.

4. Ibid., 55.

5. See Heidegger's summary of Husserl's reduction of the object of his logical investigation into an object of consciousness in his outline for "Part Two—The Phenomenological Path of the Hermeneutics of Facticity," *Ontology*, vi.

6. *Ontology.* 69.

7. Ibid., 69.

8. Ibid., 56.

9. Ibid., 58.

10. Ibid., 58–59.

11. Ibid., 59.

12. Ibid., 59.

13. Ibid., 59.

14. Ibid., 59.

15. Ibid., 59.

16. See the introduction to *Ontology.* 3.

17. See Heidegger's outline in "Part One," *Ontology.* 5.

18. *Ontology.* 13.

19. Heidegger devoted Part One of the lecture to the discussion of the idea of facticity and the concept of man.

20. *Ontology.* 9–11.

21. Ibid., 12–13.

22. Ibid., 13.

23. Ibid., 12.

24. Ibid., 11.

25. Ibid., 11.

26. Ibid., 11–12.

27. Ibid., 10.

28. Ibid., 14.

29. Ibid., 15.

30. Ibid., 12.

31. Ibid., 24.

32. Ibid., 12.

33. Ibid., 68.

34. See the English translation by Wing-Tsit Chang in his *A Source Book in Chinese Philosophy*, (New Jersey: Princeton University Press, 1963), 224.

35. See Fritjof Capra's discussion in *The Tao of Physics* (Boston: Shambhala, 1991).

36. Ibid., 24.

37. Ibid., 132–35.

38. John Clarke, *The Tao of the West* (New York, Routledge, 2000), 76.

39. *Ontology*, 14.

40. Ibid., 30.

41. Ibid., 76.

42. Ibid., 77.

43. Ibid., 77.

44. "A Dialogue on Language," in *On the Way to Language*. 33.

45. Ibid., 33.

46. Ibid., 12.

47. "The Nature of Language," in *On the Way to Language*. 104.

48. Ibid., 101.

49. "A Dialogue on Language," 19.

50. "The Nature of Language," 102.

51. Ibid., 104.

BIBLIOGRAPHY

Abe, Masao. 1995. *Buddhism and Inter-Faith Dialogue.* Edited by Steven Heine. Honolulu: University of Hawaii Press.

———. 1985. *Zen and Western Thought.* Edited by W. R. LaFleur. Honolulu: University of Hawaii Press.

Angle, Leonard. 1994. *Enlightenment: East and West.* Albany: State University of New York Press.

Balslev, Anindita N. 1996. *Cross-Cultural Conversation.* Atlanta: Scholars Press.

———. 1991. *Cultural Otherness: Correspondence with Richard Rorty.* Atlanta: Scholars Press.

Bentley, Jerry H. 1993. *Old World Encounters: Cross-Cultural Contact Exchanges in Pre-Modern Times.* Oxford: Oxford University Press.

Campbell, Mary B. 1988. *The Witness and the Other World: Exotic European Travel Writing, 400–1600.* Ithaca: Cornell University Press.

Chow, Rey. 1993. *Writing Diaspora: Tactics of Intervention in Contemporary Cultural Studies.* Bloomington: Indiana University Press.

Clarke, John. 2000. *The Tao of the West: Western Transformation of Taoist Thought.* New York: Routledge.

———. 1997. *Oriental Enlightenment: The Encounter between Asian and Western Thought.* New York: Routledge.

Clifford, James. 1988. *The Predicament of Culture: 20th Century Ethnography, Literature, and Art.* Cambridge: Harvard University Press.

Dallmayr, Fred. 1996. *Beyond Orientalism: Essays on Cross-Cultural Encounter.* Albany: State University of New York Press.

Desmond, William. 1987. *Desire, Dialectics and Otherness.* New Haven: Yale University Press.

Dreyfus, Hubert L. 1994. *Being-in-the-World: A Commentary on Heidegger's Being and Time, Division 1.* Cambridge, Massachusetts: MIT Press.

Featherstone, Mike, ed. 1990. *Global Culture: Nationalism, Globalization and Modernity.* Sage Publications.

Garfield, Jay. 2002. *Empty Words: Buddhist Philosophy and Cross-Cultural Interpretation.* Oxford: Oxford University Press.

Garrier, James, ed. 1995. *Occidentalism: Images of the West.* Oxford: Clarendon Press.

Geertz, Clifford. 1973. *The Interpretation of Cultures.* New York: Basic Books.

Gillespie, M. Michael. 1984. *Hegel, Heidegger, and the Ground of History.* Chicago: University of Chicago Press.

Goody, Jack. 1996. *The East in the West.* Cambridge: Cambridge University Press.

Gupta, Bina and Jitendranath, Mohanty, eds. 1996. *Philosophical Questions: East and West.* New York: Rowman & Littlefield.

Harasym, Sarah. 1990. *Post-Colonial Critic: Interviews, Strategies, Dialogues.* New York: Routledge.

Heidegger, Martin. 1999. *Ontology—The Hermeneutics of Facticity.* Translated by John Burn. Bloomington: Indiana University Press.

———. 1971. "The Dialogue on Language." In *On the Way to Language*, by Martin Heidegger. Translated by Peter D. Hertz. San Francisco: Harper & Row.

———. 1971. "The Nature of Language." In *On the Way to Language*, by Martin Heidegger. Translated by Peter D. Hertz. San Francisco: Harper & Row.

———. 1962. *Being and Time.* Translated by John Macquarrie and Edward Robin. San Francisco: Harper & Row.

Heim, S. Mark. 2001. *Salvations: Truth and Differences in Religion.* New York: Orbis Books.

King, Richard. 1999. *Orientalism and Religion: Postcolonial Theory, India and the Mystic East.* New York: Routledge.

Kolb, David. 1986. *The Critique of Pure Modernity.* Chicago: University of Chicago Press.

Krell, David Farrell. 1977. *Martin Heidegger: Basic Writings.* San Francisco: Harper & Row.

Larson, Gerald James and Eliot Deutsch, eds. 1988. *Interpretation Across Boundaries.* Princeton: Princeton University Press.

Nakamura, Hajime. 1964. *Ways of Thinking of Eastern Peoples.* Edited by Philip Wiener. Honolulu: University of Hawaii Press.

Needham, Joseph. 1979. *Within the Four Seas: The Dialogue of East and West.* Toronto: University of Toronto Press.

Parkes, Graham, ed. 1987. *Heidegger and Asian Thought.* Honolulu: University of Hawaii Press.

Rorty, Richard. 1982. *Consequences of Pragmatism.* Minneapolis: University of Minnesota Press.

————. 1979. *Philosophy and the Mirror of Nature.* Princeton: Princeton University Press.

Rouner, Leory, ed. 1988. *Human Rights and the World's Religions.* Notre Dame: University of Notre Dame Press.

Said, Edward. W. 1997. *Culture and Imperialism.* New York: Vantage Books.

————. 1983. *The World, the Text, and the Critic.* Cambridge: Harvard University Press.

————. 1979. *Orientalism.* New York: Vantage Books Edition.

Segesvary, Victor. 2000. *Inter-Civilizational Relations and the Destiny of the West.* Maryland: University Press of America.

Warnke, Georgia. 1987. *Gadamer: Hermeneutics, Tradition and Reason.* Stanford: Stanford University Press.

INDEX

Adhere, 105

Aesthetic category, 51, 76; and European, 55

Analects, 22

Appropriate and appropriating, 56, 57, 65, 73

Aristotle, 4

Asia 4, 5, 15, 26, 33, 36, 41, 48; tradition, 74

Balslev, Anindita N., 5, 6, 11, 12, 13, 15, 18, 19, 20, 21, 23, 25, 26, 27, 28, 29, 30, 32, 33, 41, 105

Being, 48, 69, 70, 73, 79, 80, 81, 82, 83, 84, 92, 94, 99, 101; and language 53, 54, 60, 64, 107

Being and Time, 47, 49, 51, 89

Being-in-the-world, 7, 48, 71, 83, 89, 94, 95

Being-with-the-other, 7, 65, 71, 83

Binary opposites, 79, 105, 106

Buddha Amida, 85

Buddhist and Buddhism, 25, 47, 58, 59, 100, 103; hermeneutics, 102; outlook, 90; teaching, 101, 106; and Zen, 74, 82, 84

Cartesian, 30, 104

Chinese, 21, 22, 36, 64; aesthetics, 82; religious worldviews, 59; written scripts, 62, 63

Christianity, 34, 35

Clark, John, 3, 4, 5, 104

Clifford, James, 42

Civilization, 22

Comparative philosophy, 3, 11, 12, 15, 19, 20, 23, 26, 27, 34, 47, 90

Confucianism, 25, 26

Concurrent, 100

Conversation, 21, 28, 29, 30, 31, 32, 33, 34, 47

Copenhagen Theory, 104

Cross-cultural, 18, 33, 41, 42; context, 28, 106, 53; conversation, 12, 13, 34, 65; dialogue, 51; encounter, 40, 44, 49, 61, 73, 75, 90, 103, 105, 106; hermeneutics, 67, 104; relation, 73; translation, 51; understanding, 6, 48, 81, 89, 105

Correlativity, 72

Cosmic and cosmological, 58, 59, 63, 64, 79, 81, 82, 107

Cultural hegemony, 41

Culture Otherness 11, 12, 27

Curriculum, 21, 22, 25, 27

Daoist and Daoism, 25, 47, 60, 74

Dasein, 51, 71, 89, 94, 95, 96, 97, 98, 100; and language 52

Deconstruction, 14, 17

Dependent Origination, 84, 90, 99, 100, 101, 102, 103

Derrida, 5, 17, 19, 30, 37, 43, 99

Destiny, 48, 69, 72

Dialectical totality, 37

Dialogue, 6, 11, 16, 19, 20, 25, 26, 28, 44, 47, 48, 49, 50, 51, 57, 81; of East-West, 5; on language, 67; and thinking, 57

Discipline and disciplinary, 6, 19, 21, 28, 33, 67, 90, 92, 95; of botany, 93; boundary, 35; of logic, 92

East-West, 4, 5, 6, 12, 13, 14, 36, 41, 47, 49, 85; asymmetry, 20, 25, 26, 74, 75; comparison, 15, 16, 17, 23; encounter, 3, 83, 105; relation, 7, 75, 90
Enlightenment, 3, 34, 35, 37, 38; of Sakyamuni, 99, 100
Embodiment, 78, 79, 81, 82; of thinking, 83
Emptiness, 58, 59, 60, 61, 62, 102, 103
Epistemology and epistemological, 16, 17, 18, 30, 68, 69; dualism, 90, 94, 104
Essentialism, 13, 16, 18, 19, 28, 30
Ethnocentrism, 12, 14, 23, 30, 31, 32, 33
Etymology, 58, 59, 60, 63, 90
Europe, 4, 19, 31, 32, 36
Exotic, 29, 40

Fate, 83, 85
Fa-tsang, 101, 102, 103, 106
Feminist, 40
Foucault, Michel, 37, 38, 99, 101
Fourfold world, 80, 107
Fundamentalism, 32

Germans, 48, 49; dialectics, 63, 64; word, 56
Gesture, 77, 78, 79, 81, 82
Global, 21, 25
Greek, 5, 11, 12, 14, 25, 28, 35, 36, 37 49, 91; culture and religion, 69; origin, 67, 68, 90; philosophy, 94; poetics, 57; thinking of Being, 53; word, 55; worldview, 80

Habermas, Jurgen, 31, 99
Hegel, 35, 37, 38
Hegelian dialectics, 42
Heidegger, Martin, 3, 6, 13, 14, 15, 16, 18, 19, 37, 47, 49, 50, 55, 56, 65, 89, 90, 91, 92, 101, 102, 103, 106, 107; on East-West relations, 74, 51; on hand gesture, 83; on hermeneutics, 68, 69,

76; on language, 51, 52, 53, 60, 63, 62, 64; on self, 100; on technology, 79, 80, 83, 85
Hermeneutical and hermeneutics, 48, 49, 67, 68, 71, 95; of facticity, 6, 89, 90; investigation, 94; movement, 73; relation, 70, 73; and twofold world, 71; worldviews, 72
History, 6, 35, 36, 94
Humanism, 34, 35
Husserl, Edmond, 3, 36, 49, 90, 91, 92, 93, 99

Ideology, 31
Iki, 50, 55, 68, 76
Imperialism, 22, 23
India, 22, 23, 41
Interdependence, 72
Interpretation, 48, 69
Irrationalism, 31, 32

Japanese, 21, 22, 44, 48, 84; artistic experiences, 68, 78; intellectuals, 74; poetics, 50; theater, 77; tradition, 64

Kant, 5, 29, 30, 31, 35
Karma, 83, 84, 85
Knowledge, 31, 37, 41, 68, 92, 98
Kolb, David, 73, 74, 75, 76
Koto, and *Koto ba*, 47, 54, 56, 57, 58, 59, 60, 62, 63
Kyoto School, 49

Language, 6, 30, 34, 38, 39, 47, 48, 49, 50, 51, 59, 62, 63, 65, 75; as cosmic event, 58; and East Asian, 54; as Saying 58; and technology, 53; world, 60, 61, 64
Linear time, 72, 106

Metalinguistics, 51, 52, 57, 75, 76
Metaphor, 20, 49; of language by Heidegger, 52, 53, 61
Metaphysics, and metaphysical, 14, 15, 16, 17, 18, 20, 28, 38, 50, 53, 57, 62, 74, 75, 95, 104, 105

Method and methodology, 19, 48, 68, 69; of interpretation, 67, 89
Modernization, 24, 40
Morality, 31, 32
Multiplicity, 73, 74, 105

Nihilism, 19
Noh Theater, 77, 78, 81, 83
Nothingness, 61

Object-as-perceived, 92, 93, 100
Object-in-itself, 92, 93, 100
Ontological and ontology, 6, 52, 78, 89, 97; hermeneutics, 98, 100, 101, 103; property, 58, 64, 94
Onto-cosmic origin, 65
Oriental, 4; enlightenment 3, 5; literature, 41; Orientalism, 42, 44
Other and otherness, 4, 5, 12, 13, 19, 20, 23, 25, 26, 27, 29, 32, 33, 34, 35, 37, 38, 39, 40, 41, 42, 104, 107

Parkes, Graham, 48, 60
Phenomenology, 90, 91, 92, 93, 94
Philosophy, 6, 12, 13, 14, 15, 16, 17, 18, 19, 21, 27, 28, 29, 32, 33, 34, 36, 37, 39
Plato, 14, 22, 29, 31, 37, 93, 94, 95
Postcolonial, 24, 28, 38, 41, 42, 43, 44
Postmodernism, 14, 18, 28, 30, 37, 42
Pragmatism, 11, 24, 28, 30, 38
Primordial instance, 75, 76, 78, 79, 80, 81, 99

Racism, 25
Reason, 32
Relativism, 31

Religion and religious, 12, 24, 25, 37, 81, 84, 85
Romantic, 40, 41
Representation, 42, 43, 44
Rorty, Richard, 3, 6, 11, 12, 13, 14, 15, 16, 17, 18, 19, 20, 21, 22, 23, 24, 25, 27, 28, 29, 30, 31, 33, 38, 39, 40, 41

Said, Edward, 40, 41, 42, 44
Science, 68
Secularization, 24, 25
Smith, Huston, 3
Simultaneity, 72, 78, 81, 102

Technological and technology, 3, 4, 14, 24, 25, 40, 50, 53, 62, 74, 75, 77, 79, 80, 81, 85, 104
Temporal-spatial circularity, 72, 107
Tezuka, 47, 48, 49, 50, 54, 56, 57, 58, 61, 76, 78
Theoretical, 3
Theo-metaphysical, 7, 25, 99, 100
Tradition, 25, 28, 34, 41, 49, 64, 69, 73
Translation, 6, 48, 50, 53
Twofold World, 70, 71, 76

Universal, 31; humanity, 36
Upanishads, 22

West, 4, 5, 13, 14, 15, 16, 17, 18, 19, 20, 21, 23, 25, 28, 32
World-encounter, 6, 89, 103
World history 35, 36, 39
Worldviews, 89, 98
World Wars, 18, 25

Zhuang Ze, 82